150 NEW BEST OF THE BEST HOUSE IDEAS

150 NEW BEST OF THE BEST HOUSE IDEAS

MACARENA ABASCAL VALDENEBRO

HARPER
DESIGN
An Imprint of HarperCollins Publishers

150 NEW BEST OF THE BEST HOUSE IDEAS
Copyright © 2020 by LOFT Publications

HarperCollins books may be purchased for educational, business, or sales promotional use.
For information, please email the Special Markets Department at SPsales@harpercollins.com.

First published in 2020 by
Harper Design
An Imprint of HarperCollinsPublishers
195 Broadway
New York, NY 10007
Tel.: (212) 207-7000
Fax: (855) 746-6023
harperdesign@harpercollins.com
www.hc.com

Distributed throughout the world by
HarperCollinsPublishers
195 Broadway
New York, NY 10007

Editorial coordinator: Claudia Martínez Alonso
Art director: Mireia Casanovas Soley
Editor and texts: Macarena Abascal Valdenebro
Layout: Cristina Simó Perales

ISBN 978-0-06-301885-3

Library of Congress Control Number: 2020017940

Printed in Malaysia
First printing, 2020

CONTENTS

INTRODUCTION

Throughout history, the construction of houses has been a faithful mirroring of the people´s lifestyle living in them, of their uses and traditions, and therefore it has been in constant change.

In recent years there has been a revolution in the world of interior design and housing architecture. Designers and architects are striving to create welcoming homes that reflect the personality of their residents, retreats of well-being. We want places where we can feel good, where we can have a part of ourselves in the space around us, environments that reveal our feelings or our way of understanding life. We continue to create spaces where simplicity prevails, but in this search for character, designers play with contrasts of styles, textures, materials, colors, and also the contrast between the old and the new.

Changes in both our way of life and in family structures give rise to open-plan dwellings where living spaces flow into each other, changing their configuration easily through the use of sliding doors or panels, integrating the different atmospheres of the house. In most cases, the kitchen, dining room, and living room merge into a whole that helps to ensure greater communication and interaction between those who live in the house.

The search for bright spaces is the main requirement when building or remodeling a house. That is why dwellings usually have skylights, interior patios or large windows, which can sometimes replace the walls, turning these homes into large everyday windows. However, as many of them are located in the middle of nature, there are no problems of lack of privacy; on the contrary, they allow you to enjoy the beauty of the surrounding landscapes without the need to leave home.

Respect for the environment is also a priority in housing construction; its designs are increasingly adapted to their surroundings and are governed by sustainability criteria. The use of recyclable materials or materials obtained from local raw sources, as well as the consolidation of technologies that use renewable energies (such as photovoltaic solar panels or others that reduce water consumption or make use of rainwater for different uses) are some of the measures that are usually adopted to comply with these criteria.

Nowadays we value the conservation of our environment and the heritage that can perfectly coexist with the present if it is done in an adequate way. We rehab houses with the desire to improve living conditions and comfort, to adapt them to our new way of life, without losing their essence. Sometimes the aim is to increase the useful surface area by taking advantage of the space of a patio or a garden, or adding a new floor on top or an extension. This requires an important work of creativity by the architect to harmoniously fuse the old and the new.

All of this is reflected in the pages of this book where projects of single-family homes of different typologies are shown—new or rehabilitated, houses in the city, in the countryside, in the mountains, surrounded by a lush forest or facing the sea—offering intelligent and ingenious construction and design solutions with a careful aesthetic and with the aim of respecting the environment adapting to the surroundings in which they have been built.

Clinging to the slopes of Camelback Mountain in Phoenix, Arizona, this former Spanish Colonial Revival–style home, the decorative style of which was not taking advantage of the natural environment, has been transformed into the Red Rocks residence, a home that creates a variety of experiences with both natural and man-made environments. Superfluous decorations and design elements were avoided, leaving a simple two-story stucco box. The floor plan was reorganized to prioritize the connection between the living spaces and the views, including a new steel, glass, and wood staircase that allows a view from the back of the house through the front and beyond the valley.

Red Rocks
4,491 sq ft

The Ranch Mine
Phoenix, Arizona, United States
© Roehner + Ryan

001

The first floor covered patio, accessed by a custom pivot gate by Bang Bang Designs, is lined with misters to keep the space cool all year round in the desert heat and to transition the open living space to hot tub and firepit and down to the pool area.

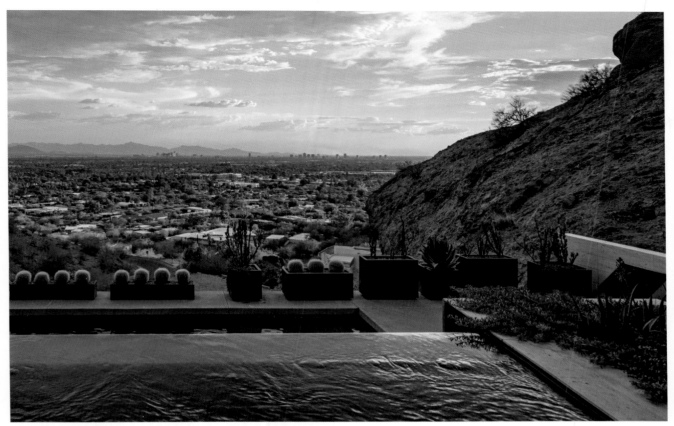

Existing second floor plan

Renovated second floor plan

Existing first floor plan

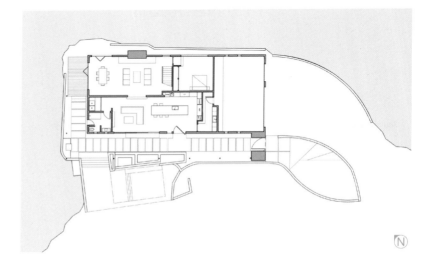

Renovated first floor plan

1

2

3

4

Diagrams

1. Existing Spanish Colonial Revival-style house
2. Strip back heavy stylistic elements repressing site potential
3. Retain the existing two-story frame as the building block
4. Extend living spaces to fully take advantage of the site and its views

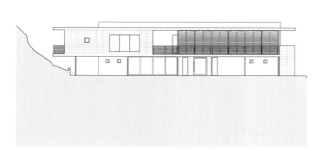

Southwest elevation

Northwest elevation

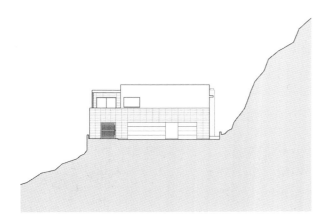

Southeast elevation

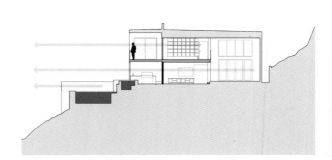

Building section

002

Concrete was poured onto the first
floor while maple wood lumber
was kept for the second floor. A
fairly neutral palette of walnut and
white cabinetry with a variety of
quartz counters and marble tile
were used throughout to keep the
red rocks as the star material.

003

The use of the color white and the design of the library favor spatial continuity and facilitate the room's absolute integration into the environment. The color accents come from the books and decorative objects, which add dynamism.

004

Over 2,000 square feet of shaded exterior patios were created, extending the living space of the house in every direction and providing shade for the interior spaces.

005

The large south-facing second
floor patio, with an Ipe ceiling and
floor, features bifold custom steel
screens that help shield the deck
from the harsh desert sun while
still allowing the breeze to come
through but can be folded aside at
dusk to take in the famous Arizona
sunsets.

006

Mirrors were floated above the master bathroom vanity in front of the mountain's face to visually anchor the home to its unique site.

This house is located on a finite plot in an open and green environment. The main challenge of the project was to create an architectural strategy that dialogues with the material and the light as opposed to a traditional approach to a compact layout.

The house is organized in two floors. On the ground floor, the public spaces are located in direct relation with the garden, linking in a dynamic way with a wooden joint that acts as a nucleus, articulating the space between both levels. On the upper floor are the private spaces in connection with the garden terrace, which operates as a viewpoint for contemplating nature.

Casa DAB

2,368 sq ft covered area
+ 430 sq ft semi-covered area

BAM! Arquitectura

Buenos Aires, Argentina
© Federico Cairoli

007

Sustainability is approached from all levels: the choice of the land, its implementation, the installation of a green roof, the use of rainwater for irrigation, the low-consumption appliances, and the use of geothermal energy to cool the interiors.

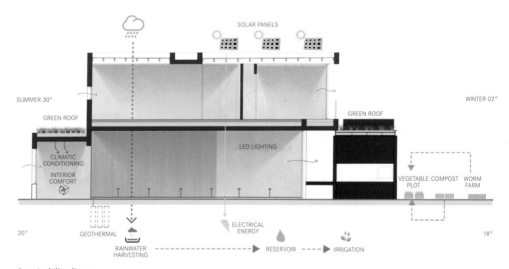

SOLAR PANELS

SUMMER 30°

WINTER 02°

GREEN ROOF

GREEN ROOF

CLIMATIC CONDITIONING

LED LIGHTING

INTERIOR COMFORT

VEGETABLE PLOT · COMPOST · WORM FARM

20°

18°

GEOTHERMAL

ELECTRICAL ENERGY

RAINWATER HARVESTING → RESERVOIR → IRRIGATION

Sustainability diagram

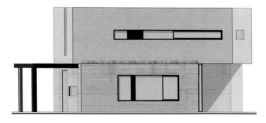

Front elevation

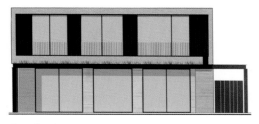

Rear elevation

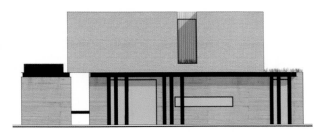

Left elevation

Right elevation

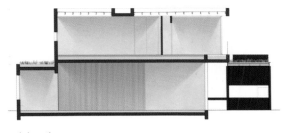

A-A section

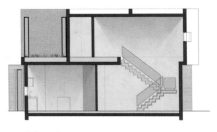

B-B section

The landscape was designed on sustainable premises and offers a great contribution to urban ecology from the use of native species, thus building an urban micro patch formed by native plant communities.

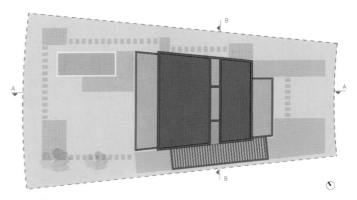

Roof plan

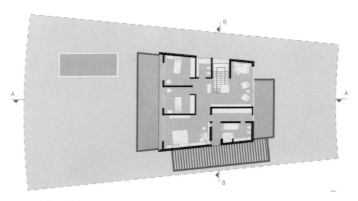

First floor plan

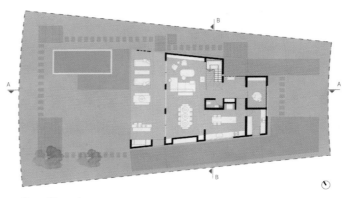

Ground floor plan

008

The fusion of materials was key
in order to generate a sensory
journey throughout. A brick
structure rests on a concrete base.
A double space with a wooden
core links the two levels. The last
element is the iron, used in the
parasols, that acts as a filter to
regulate the entrance of light into
the spaces.

009

In the living area, large glass enclosures were installed, allowing light to flood the space and providing a direct connection with nature.

010

All the spaces were designed to be illuminated with natural light, to have views to the outside, and to be cross-ventilated; a benefit not only energetic but of greater comfort for its environment. To protect from the strong northern and western sun, iron parasols were installed on the upper floor.

This sculptural, light-filled house, the form and planning of which were inspired in part by the owners' Brazilian and Moroccan heritages, offers an alternative to the mostly conventional structures of the surrounding neighborhood. Mirroring the subtle differentiation between public and private spaces within the house, the exterior changes from front (street) to back. Whereas the street side of the house incorporates highly regulated, two-dimensional curved volumes that are subdued in character, their pent-up energy explodes in an exuberant composition of three-dimensional curved volumes at the rear, where the interior opens generously to the exterior and the forms express a more contemporary, open, and transparent global culture that embraces complexity as well as the natural environment.

Casa Namorada
4,200 sq ft

JFAK
Santa Monica, California, United States

© Benny Chan, Fotoworks

A pergola of gently undulating powder-coated aluminum slats provides shelter from the sun on the concrete back terrace.

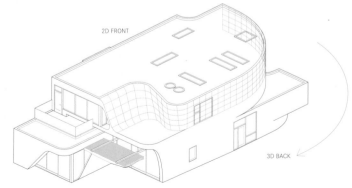

2D FRONT

3D BACK

Building surface diagram

There is a gradient of "public" to "private" space that runs from front to back. A long hallway separates a formal living room just inside the front door, where less familiar guests are met and entertained, from the dining and family rooms toward the rear of the house.

011

The skylights ensure that light enters the space even on the chilliest days. They enhance the space and give a greater feeling of spaciousness.

Second level plan

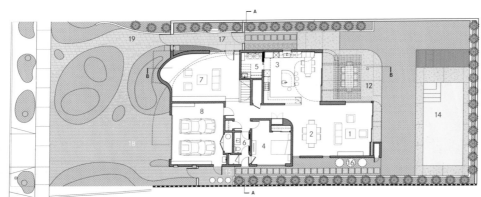

1. Family room	12. Closet
2. Dining room	13. Bedroom
3. Kitchen	14. Pool
4. Guest bedroom	15. Trash
5. Laundry	16. Compost
6. Bathroom	17. Entrance
7. Living room	courtyard
8. Garage	18. Driveway
9. Terrace	19. Walkway
10. Master bedroom	20. Patio
11. Master bathroom	

First level plan

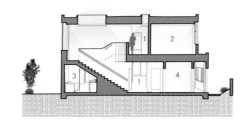

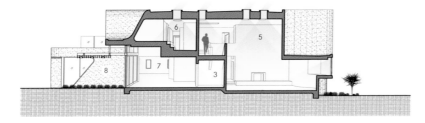

1. Hall	6. Master
2. Bedroom	bathroom
3. Laundry	7. Kitchen
4. Bathroom	8. Patio
5. Living room	

Sections

36 Casa Namorada

The rich rear portion of the house is as open and curvilinear as its more sober front facade is closed and rectilinear.

012

Throughout all spaces, there is minimal detail and an emphasis on the quality of space and light. Both inside and outside, fluid forms and curves, many of them activated by natural light, reference the organic forms commonly found in Brazil.

013

Splashes of color and texture in furnishings create an environment that is simultaneously minimal and warm, abstract and intimate.

In the master bathroom, blue waves suggest the urban landscapes of Burle Marx, while the children's bathrooms are patterned with geometric soccer balls.

The design of this house, situated on a lot of Di Lido Island with superb views, draws on the jet-set lifestyle of Biscayne Bay to evoke the experience of being on the deck of a luxurious yacht. Multiple events unfold on this versatile terrace whose defining characteristic—the harmonious merging of internal and external living spaces—is a theme carried throughout the house.

The entrance from the street is more restrained. Once inside, the splayed nature of the site becomes apparent as the rooms pull apart to form a dramatic canyon whose volume frames the view out into the bay. All the principal living spaces look out onto a semi-covered collection of external living rooms situated on the verge of the curved arc of the bay.

Di Lido

17,975 sq ft

SAOTA

Miami, Florida, United States

© Adam Letch

014

Deep, covered outdoor spaces characterize the rear yard of the property. With the seamless transitions from indoor-outdoor, the versatility of the space ensures the Miami weather can be enjoyed throughout the year.

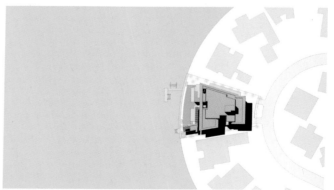

Site plan

015

Conceived as the back of a super yacht, the outdoor spaces epitomize the notion of living on the water in Miami.

Transitions from indoor to terrace to the bay are purposefully downplayed.

The upper bedroom level houses the sea-facing master suite, complete with hot tub and pool, and three on-the-water suites created for the owner's three daughters.

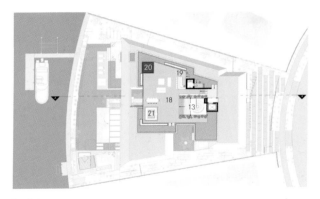

Roof plan

First floor plan

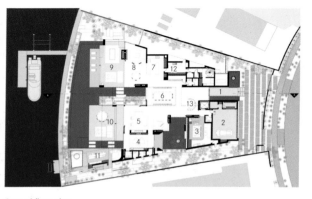

Ground floor plan

1. Entrance
2. Garage
3. Cinema
4. Study
5. Great room
6. Dining room
7. Kitchen
8. Family room
9. Family terrace
10. Pool terrace
11. Pool bar
12. Butler kitchen
13. Stairwell
14. Double height
15. Bedroom
16. Gym
17. Staff bed
18. Roof terrace
19. Roof bar
20. Hot tub
21. Firepit

Lush planting lines a generous in-out driveway, and a series of wall planes and volumes, held together by a curved screen of etched glass, signal a grand, double-height entrance hall.

016

An interior courtyard with koi pond
and vertical garden gives rise to an
outdoor space that is both intimate
and serene.

017

Elements of bronze "jewels" have been added to add texture to the interiors. Suspended screens give a certain privacy to the dining room without breaking the continuity of the space.

The sculptural staircase becomes the focal point of the space. A rich and sophisticated tension is created in the contrast of the material palette and the vivid, rich landscape.

018

Limestone, hand-picked in Portugal, and chocolate browns—wood, leather, and bronze—define the interior palette, whose uniformity is subtly broken by the cushioned fabrics or the hanging works of art.

Built on a large pie-shaped cul-de-sac, this Eichler home remodel starts with one of the nicer tepee models. The architect's primary approach was to leverage and improve upon the already significant indoor-outdoor aspects of the house, as well as enlarging most of the smaller rooms, while preserving views from all spaces. A major improvement to the original design involved opening up the kitchen/breakfast nook to views of the pool and yard by adding multi-slide doors and removing an oddly placed laundry room. Rotating the kitchen 90 degrees to an interior wall improved the flow. The design team of architect, landscape architect, and interior designer joined forces with the general contractor, Pete Moffat Construction, to upgrade the house to the clients' specifications while maintaining its original mid-century spirit.

Late-vintage Eichler Remodel
3,434 sq ft

Guy and Ian Ayers/Moody Studio, Ground Studio, Jeanne Moeschler Interior Design, and Pete Moffat Construction

Los Altos, California, United States

© David Duncan Livingston

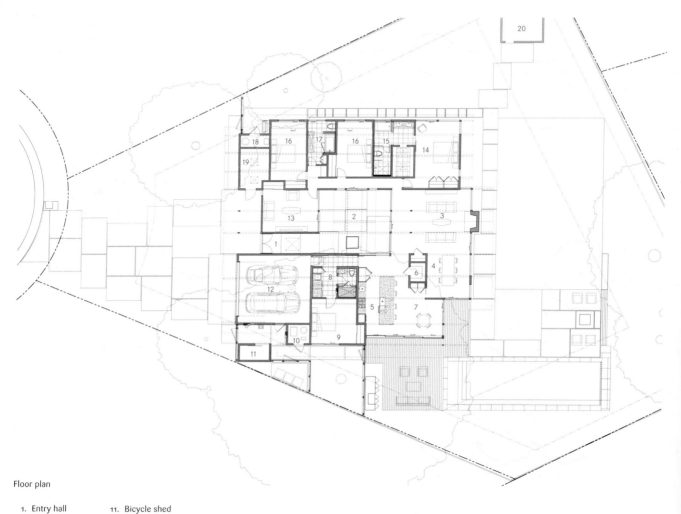

Floor plan

1. Entry hall
2. Atrium
3. Living room
4. Dining room
5. Kitchen
6. Pantry
7. Nook
8. Laundry
9. Guest bedroom
10. Pool equipment
11. Bicycle shed
12. Garage
13. Family den
14. Master bedroom
15. Master bathroom
16. Bedroom
17. Bathroom
18. Mechanical room
19. Storage
20. Office shed

West elevation

The house embodies iconic features of the mid-century modern homes developed by Joseph Eichler, who promoted affordable post-and-beam construction, generous use of exposed wood, and connection with the outdoors.

East elevation

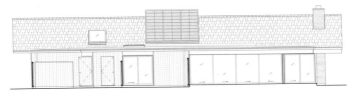

South elevation

North elevation

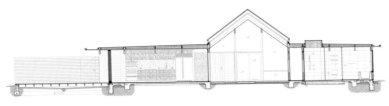

Building section

Site plan

A. Main house
B. Garage

1a. Concrete paving
1b. Timber decking
1c. Gravel paving
2. Timber bench and
   concrete seat wall
3. Firepit

4. Pool
5. Water feature
6. BBQ and
   enclosure
7. Office shed
8. Mailbox

NORTH

Late-vintage Eichler Remodel

019

Outdoor spaces can act as extensions of indoor rooms. An interior floor that is flush with the exterior deck enhances the connection between the indoors and the outdoors.

The renovation stays true to the Eichler home spirit, highlighting lofty gabled ceilings and floor-to-ceiling windows that allow in abundant natural light. Sophisticated furnishings never compete with the architecture, but emphasize indoor-outdoor living using natural tones and organic shapes.

020

A simple and understated selection of finishes and furnishings contributes to the creation of a timeless design. In this case, the owners desired a California coastal influence in the home, interpreted through felled stone, rich wood, earthen tones, and handmade finishes.

021

Deep eaves protect outer walls
and windows from harsh sunlight,
maintaining a pleasant indoor
temperature.

All the bedrooms and baths were enlarged into the side yards—relatively easy to do structurally, perpendicular to the beam span direction—while still maintaining the substantial side-yard landscaping.

022

The major benefit that comes with skylights is the extra natural light. Some designs are operable, allowing airflow and improving ventilation. On the other hand, skylights can create heat gain problems when they are not placed adequately, taking into account orientation and size.

This project consists of the renovation and addition to a 1950s post-and-beam house situated within an established forest environment in West Vancouver.

The existing house was stripped of layers of past renovation and restored to a modern-day version of its former self, with the existing timber structure and form remaining largely intact. To accommodate functions that were absent in the original, a new addition was designed to the east of the house, representing a formal departure from the original post-and-beam structure, both in terms of scale and materiality. With its dark-stained cedar siding, green roof, and surrounding native landscape, the house seeks to become a natural extension of the landscape, suggestive of a mossy outcropping within the forest.

Creek House
5,000 sq ft

splyce design

West Vancouver,
British Columbia, Canada

© Sama Jim Canzian

The addition is a simple form, grounded with a dark exterior that is slightly off-axis from the original, marking the clear boundary between the two at the rear of the house.

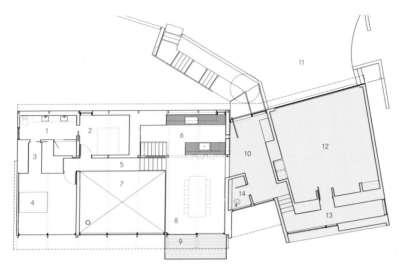

Upper floor plan

1. Bathroom	8. Dining
2. Flex Room	9. Deck
3. Dressing room	10. Entry
4. Bedroom	11. Driveway
5. Catwalk	12. Garage
6. Kitchen	13. Mudroom
7. Open to below	14. Powder room

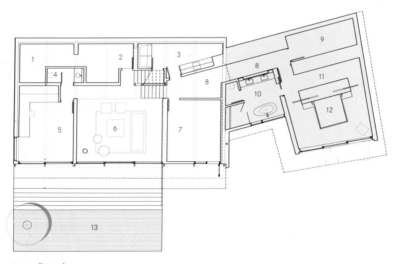

Lower floor plan

1. Mechanical	9. Storage/
2. Storage	Mechanical
3. Laundry	10. Bathroom
4. Powder room	11. Dressing
5. Office	room
6. Living room	12. Master
7. Gym	Bedroom
8. Hallway	13. Deck

023

Thanks to the architect's design, the house, far from affecting the ecosystem or violently disrupting it, is perfectly adapted and integrated into nature

The interior is simple and clean with
a focus on the outdoors. A simple
material palette flows throughout: cedar
ceilings, white oak furniture, and white
walls.

024

The exposed bolts and steel plates of the post-to-beam connections or the 1/2" steel plate ribbon stair become experiential moments in the space, adding pages to the home's seventy-year-old story.

The lush forest serves as a backdrop for this modern, sober, and minimalist kitchen and adds a note of color to the whole.

025

This division of the two volumes is pronounced on the interior with a subtle change in floor elevation and floor treatment. Two steps define the edge between the concrete floor of the addition and the new wood floor of the renovation.

026

The nobility of a material like concrete gives the feeling of durability and low maintenance that, combined with the wood and an attentive design to detail, generates a warm and cozy space.

The homeowners saw the property's unique potential and enlisted Jamie L. Brewster McLeod to transform it into a gallery for their extensive art collection.

The renovation focused on keeping the simple, elegant feeling of the original structure while using modern elements to bring in more light and enhance the mountain views. The biggest impact on the space was achieved by raising the roof in the living room, which doubled the room's height, gave it a butterfly roof, and added larger windows. Additional design elements throughout the renovation were driven by the homeowner's art collection and the desire to maintain the character of the original structure.

Maroon Creek
5,500 sq ft

Brewster McLeod Architects
Aspen, Colorado, United States
© David Patterson

027

The original fireplace, a focal point of the house, was refinished in board form concrete to enhance the modern feeling.

Upper level plan

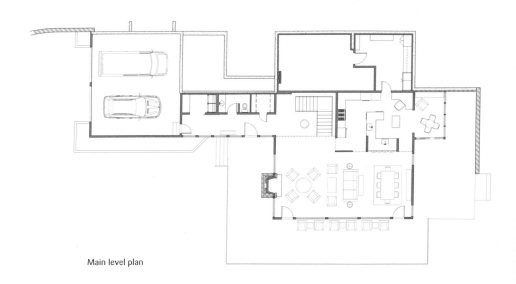

Main level plan

The coexistence between the rustic and the modern is reflected in the design of the furniture and the material used.

028

The stairway was designed around a striking collection of black-and-white photographs, while the master bedroom was redesigned around an original art piece that was purchased with the property.

029

In this children's bedroom, with capacity for eight, the wallpaper with tree trunk design, the bunk beds, and the wooden walls create the illusion of sleeping in a forest cabin.

The renovation of a 1905 Victorian house was conceived as a progression from traditional design elements to contemporary ones as one moves from public to private spaces. The Victorian facade remains intact and the rooms at the front of the house maintain all the original details. The back of the main level—originally containing a kitchen, living room, and dining room—was opened up into a single space that blends some of the existing Victorian elements with a modern kitchen and a sleek steel-and-glass balcony and staircase that connects with the backyard below, a new lush garden oasis. The living space was expanded into the garden level, which was previously basement space behind the garage. The expansion allows for a spacious modern master suite with generous closets and a Zen-like spa bathroom.

Castro Victorian
3,100 sq ft

Diego Pacheco Design Practice

San Francisco, California, United States

© Christopher Stark and Caitlin Atkinson

Renovated main floor plan

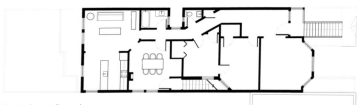

Original main floor plan

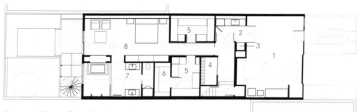

Renovated lower floor plan

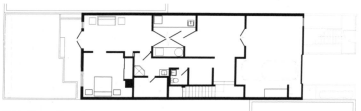

Original lower floor plan

1. Garage
2. Mudroom
3. Washer/dryer
4. Wine cellar
5. Closet
6. Mechanical
7. Master bathroom
8. Master bedroom
9. Foyer
10. Parlor
11. Guest room
12. Office
13. Great room

Small outdoor spaces can be just as enjoyable as large ones. From interesting plantings to compact furniture arrangements, these small patios or yards can transform a home into a stylish, cozy retreat.

Spiral staircases are as space-efficient as they are sleek—worth using as a focal point.

In the kitchen, European fumed-chestnut cabinetry combine with Calacatta countertops to achieve a modern, timeless aesthetic. The new baseboards, window trim, and picture rail were recreated from original 1905 detailing.

032

Variation in color, texture, and pattern creates visual interest. The key to an efficient result is in a well-balanced combination of these elements.

Rift-cut black-finish white oak wall paneling and doors provide visual richness in contrast with the stark white surfaces, achieving an elegant and simple backdrop for a thought-out selection of artwork and modern furnishings.

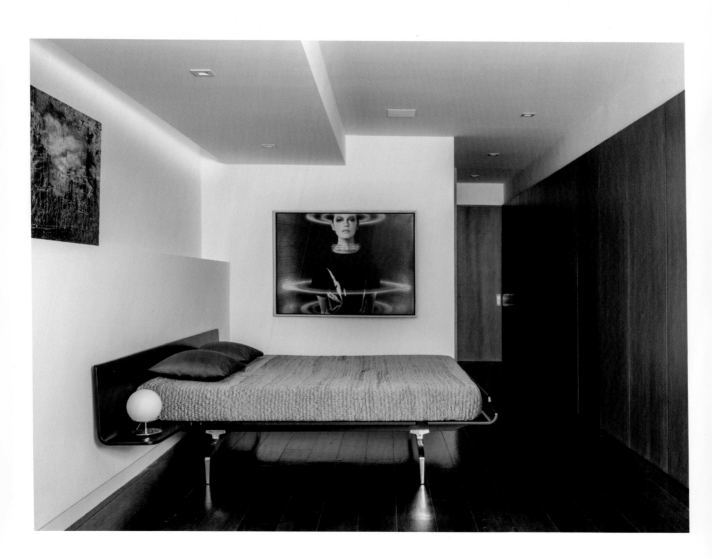

033

Neutral tones, state-of-mind lights,
a soaking tub, towel warmers, and
a massage therapy showerhead
create a soothing ambience worthy
of a spa.

This is a large addition and alterations project, restoring an existing heritage-listed 1890s three-story "Victorian Italianate-style Terrace House with Carriageway" into a brave, modern home. The underlying challenge was to transform the current 1990s office into a contemporary residence, honoring the historic style with its charming features while updating with modern comforts.

The design generates a sense of wonder and awe both inside and out, encouraging the young, growing family to explore and enjoy the various spaces with multiple sensory experiences and emotions. They are spaces of silence and contemplation, with calming and restrained aesthetics that will serve the young family well into the twenty-first century.

Italianate House
5,274 sq ft

Renato D'Ettorre Architects

Surry Hills, Sydney, Australia

© justinalexanderphoto

This house represents a dialogue between the structure and the rich context of the site, characterized as rustic charm with the new work, creating a relationship between the warmth of the old materials and the simplicity of the modern.

Street elevation

Stable front elevation

Section A

Section B

034

The glass cabinets provide visual lightness and a sense of space in addition to functioning as stylish showcases.

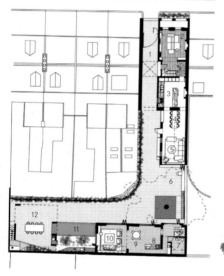

Ground floor plan

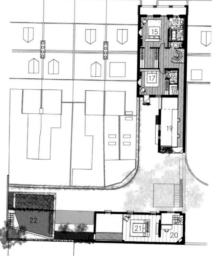

First floor plan

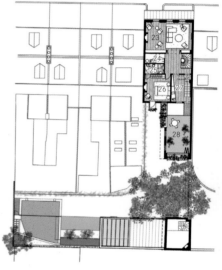

Second floor plan

1. Carriageway	8. Kitchen	15. Master bedroom	22. Roof garden
2. Living room	9. Dining room	16. Ensuite 2	23. Lounge room
3. Kitchen	10. Poolside lounge	17. Bedroom 2	24. Laundry
4. Dining room	11. Pool	18. Linen	25. Ensuite 3
5. Family room	12. Outdoor dining	19. Study	26. Bedroom 3
6. Courtyard	13. Guest powder room	20. Study	27. Kitchenette
7. Bathroom	14. Master ensuite	21. Bedroom 4	28. Conservatory

035

The bold design of a studio under the impressive original double-height brick vault ceiling, located in the rear wing, shows that without losing any of its essence, spaces can be reinterpreted to make them more functional and adapted to modern life.

036

The predominance of white,
the design of the new elements
and structures, which is sober
with pure lines, and the choice
of furniture that is simple and
without superfluous ornaments,
manage to give prominence to the
architecture and original elements.

037

The absence of doors favors the integration of the covered terrace into the dwelling and allows the light that enters through the glass roof to flow freely through the whole space, reaching the deepest corners.

038

The wooden floor with herringbone slats gives a stately style to the house. But this floor also transmits a dynamism that enriches the rooms from their base.

This home is a remodel of an existing 1970s house in Bel Air. On the client's instruction to expunge all traces of the original Spanish-style architecture, the existing house was stripped back to its timber skeleton to maximize the square footage and, by extending where necessary, create generous openings to draw in the beautiful West Coast light, and expose the rolling vistas and the verdant setting. The reconfigured floor plan aims to capture the essence of Californian living, with internal spaces feeling light, fresh, and open, connecting the various functions of the house for modern family living and grand entertaining alike. The existing house has been utterly transformed into a home that establishes a fresh contemporary aesthetic in the tradition of Californian modernism.

Stradella
13,282 sq ft

SAOTA

Los Angeles, California, United States

© Adam Letch

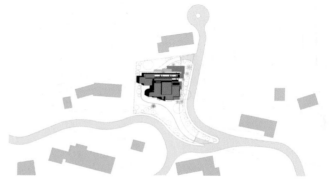

Site plan

039

A generous new linear canopy amplifies the width of the site, creating a natural extension of the internal living spaces, improving flow between the various functions of the house, and providing comfortable spaces for outdoor dining and lounging.

First floor plan

1. Horizon terrace
2. Shower
3. BBQ
4. Outdoor lounge
5. Sun terrace
6. WC
7. AV
8. Skyline bar
9. Daybeds
10. Hot tub
11. Home theater
12. Games lounge
13. Covered dining
14. Great room
15. Solarium
16. Den
17. Fireplace
18. Data
19. Cigar Bar
20. Dining
21. Cloaks
22. WC
23. Study
24. Kitchen
25. Breakfast bar
26. Entrance hall

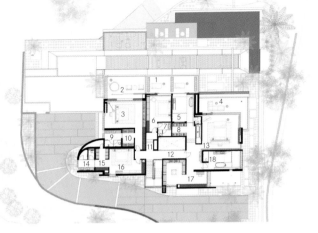

Second floor plan

1. Terrace
2. Bedroom 2 terrace
3. Bedroom 2 (guest suite)
4. Master bedroom terrace
5. Ensuite (his)
6. Bedroom 3
7. Ensuite 3
8. Dressing room his
9. Ensuite 2
10. Dresser
11. Storage
12. Gallery
13. Master bedroom
14. Ensuite 4
15. Dresser
16. Bedroom 4
17. Ensuite (hers)
18. Dressing room hers

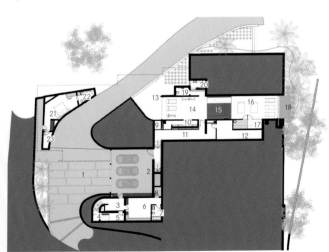

Basement plan

1. Driveway
2. Garage
3. Lobby
4. Staircase
5. Electrical cupboard
6. Staff and laundry
7. Bathroom
8. Linen closet
9. Closet
10. Cellar
11. Wine display
12. Plant room
13. Zen garden
14. Gym
15. Pool
16. Spa
17. Sauna/Steam
18. Terrace
19. Gym WC
20. Gym shower
21. Staff bedroom
22. Staff ensuite
23. Staff closet

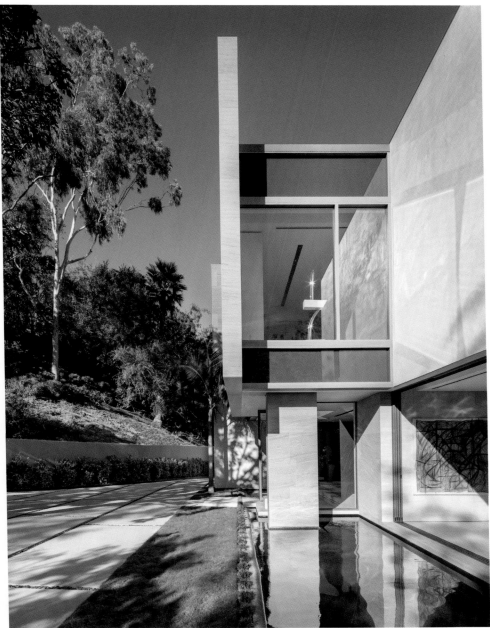

Landscaping was designed to enhance the already luxuriant setting. It was impossible to introduce a courtyard into the heart of the plan, and so the planted spaces were critical, softening the look and feel of the contemporary forms and allowing a more intimate experience of the leafy site.

The overall palette balances warm and natural tones against the bold masses and crisp linear forms that characterize the architecture. An elegant canvas of French limestone and white plaster walls is enlivened inside and out by bronze anodized aluminium screens and light gray window frames

040

Carefully designed lighting
accentuates the architecture and
responds directly to furniture
layouts, ensuring that a sense of
intimacy is established throughout
the open spaces. Concealed
fixtures and discreet layouts create
a comfortable nighttime ambience;
the twinkling LA skyline remains
the star attraction.

041

Where possible, walls were
replaced by floor-to-ceiling glazing
with sliding windows pocketing
or stacking to create generous
openings.

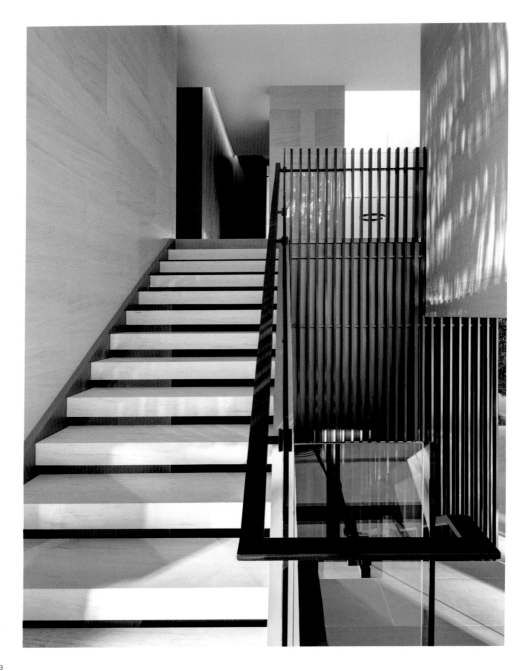

Gray-washed ash millwork and doors
complement both the limestone floor
tiles used throughout the living spaces
and the oak flooring in the bedrooms.

Casa FLD
6,000 sq ft

57STUDIO

Las Condes, Santiago, Chile

© 57STUDIO / Sergio Pirrone

The home is located in a Santiago de Chile neighborhood, in the Andean foothills where the climate is dry and warm during most of the year. Viewed from the street, the property presents a smooth slope ascending toward the mountains.

The goal was to build a single-story home that would occupy much of the property. The structure features three intersecting wings on different levels that follow the shape of the slope. This intersecting placement creates three patios and various orientations that define the location of the rooms based on their use and need for natural light.

042

The roofs were designed to provide broad spaces and generous eaves to cover the terraces and protect the interior spaces from the sun. A light, wide-span construction system allowed for the incorporation of installations and generated ventilation through the thickness of the roof, which lowers the inside temperature during the summer months.

043

When the windows are open, the boundaries between inside and outside disappear. The porches and the garden become extensions of the house itself. It is important that there is absolute harmony in the design of the different spaces.

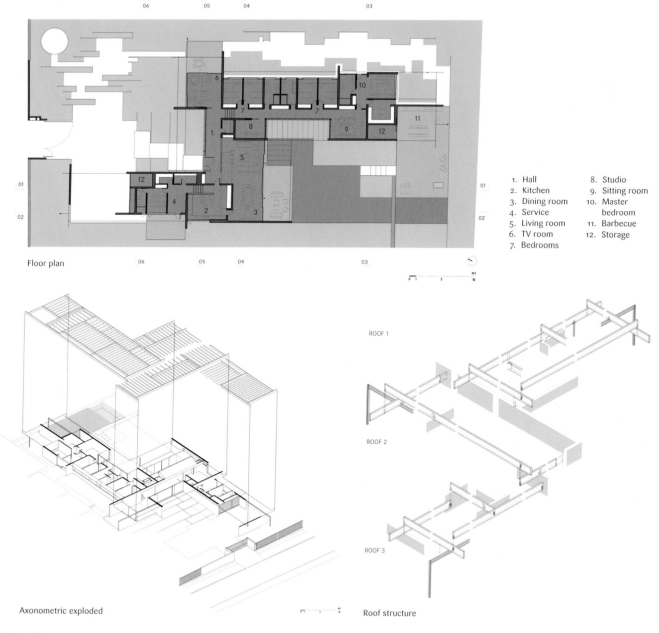

Floor plan

1. Hall
2. Kitchen
3. Dining room
4. Service
5. Living room
6. TV room
7. Bedrooms
8. Studio
9. Sitting room
10. Master bedroom
11. Barbecue
12. Storage

Axonometric exploded

ROOF 1

ROOF 2

ROOF 3

Roof structure

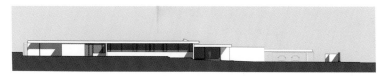

West elevation

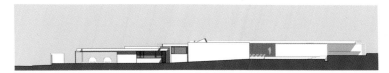

East elevation

Section 01

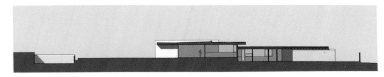

Section 02

Section 03

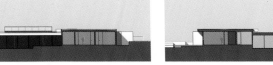

Section 04

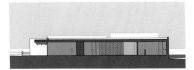

Section 05

Section 06

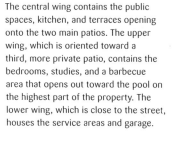

The central wing contains the public spaces, kitchen, and terraces opening onto the two main patios. The upper wing, which is oriented toward a third, more private patio, contains the bedrooms, studies, and a barbecue area that opens out toward the pool on the highest part of the property. The lower wing, which is close to the street, houses the service areas and garage.

044

Just like the flowers in the garden, the play of colors on the dining room chairs gives the room a more casual air and highlights the harmony and integration between the interior and exterior.

045

The wings have reinforced concrete walls that are staggered to delineate each structure, defining the orientations and supporting the three wooden roofs. Laminated radiata pinewood was used, which is an abundant, easily renewable resource.

046

In the exterior spaces, the structure is exposed, combining solar and ventilation control solutions based on each orientation. Radiata pinewood also was used in the windows, reinforcing the idea of contrasting the lightness of the wood with the weight of the concrete.

This 6,000-square-foot home terraces down a steep sloped lot in Tiburon with striking and unobstructed views of the bay. The material palette is an elegant combination of bright white stucco, teak, and gray limestone, with the street-facing facade featuring a dramatic teak screen.

The living spaces open up to the views, and the large decks and cantilevered terraces allow for ample outdoor living. Water is a prominent feature of this home, beginning with a waterfall at the entry that becomes a narrow water feature running directly through the public living areas and out to the pool facing the bay.

Cheng-Brier House
6,000 sq ft

Swatt I Miers Architects

Tiburon, California,
United States

© Marion Brenner,
   Russell Abraham,
   Jacob Elliott

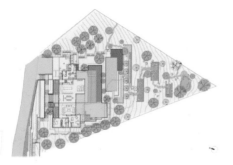

Landscape

1. Japanese bath (onsen) in courtyard
2. Wood screening on north facade for privacy

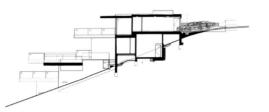

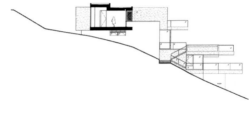

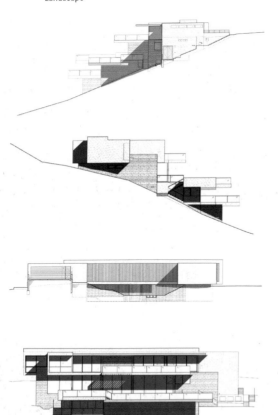

Elevations

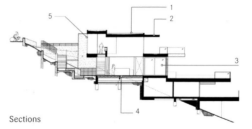

Sections

1. Solar-ready roof
2. Deep south-facing overhangs
3. Floor-to-ceiling doors for inside-outside living
4. Radiant flooring
5. Wood screening on north facade for privacy

047

The house is organized in three levels that adapt to the hillside. The entrance and all the public spaces—kitchen, dining room, living room, and family spaces—are on the middle level, accessed by stairs from the east and west ends of the property.

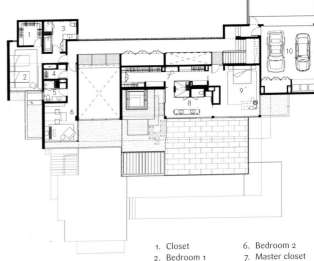

Upper floor plan

1. Closet
2. Bedroom 1
3. Bathroom 3
4. Closet
5. Bathroom 4

6. Bedroom 2
7. Master closet
8. Master bathroom
9. Master bedroom
10. Garage

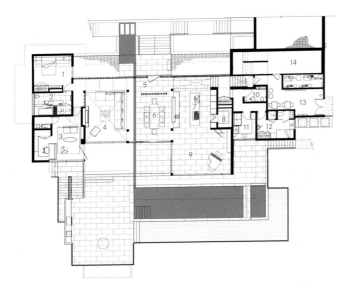

Main floor plan

1. Guest room
2. Bathroom
3. Office
4. Living room
5. Entry
6. Dining room
7. Kitchen
8. Pantry

9. Family room
10. Powder room
11. Laundry
12. Maid room
13. Pool equip./
    Mech. room
14. Crawlspace

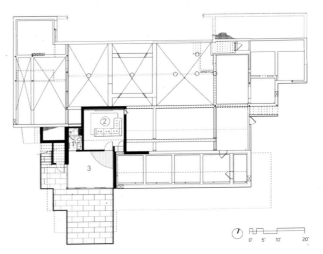

Lower floor plan

1. Bathroom 2
2. Media room
3. Exercise/pool room

048

A double-height living area adds
drama to the special interior
composition.

When it gets dark, the illuminated water tunnel becomes a focal point while accentuating the feeling of continuity between the interior and the exterior.

049

Landscape features include a pool with cantilevered decks in the middle level, connected to an entrance waterfall by a narrow interior and exterior water tunnel that slices through the home.

050

All the levels of the house are deep
cantilevered terraces on the south
side, which extend the interior
spaces to the exterior, creating
outdoor living areas from which to
enjoy the most beautiful views of
the San Francisco Bay area.

Family bedrooms are located on the upper level, with the master suite featuring a private outdoor Japanese onsen open-air bathing area that overlooks San Francisco Bay.

Located on a steep and technically challenging site in West Vancouver, the Sunset House is designed to capture immediate views of heavy marine traffic and the open sea to the west. The irregular shape of the site's boundaries align with the edge of the house and culminate in a substantial blinder, which provides privacy from adjacent properties.

Movement through the house is choreographed to disguise a considerable elevation change from the street to the main living spaces. No individual stair run is greater than one half-story. This split-level arrangement coupled with the consolidation of the upper floor to one side of the building allows for generously tall main living spaces and a close connection between upper and main floors.

Sunset House
4,979 sq ft

**McLeod Bovell
Modern Houses**

West Vancouver,
British Columbia, Canada

© Ema Peter and Martin Tessler

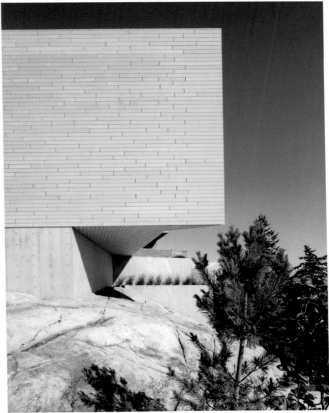

051

Concrete, Resysta, and Accoya—an engineered wood with protective treatment that is resistant to any environment—were used for the exterior finish.

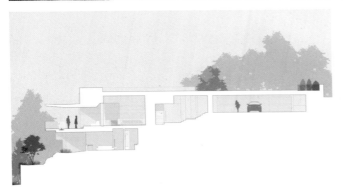

Section

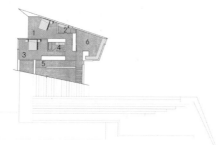

Upper floor plan

1. Bedroom
2. Ensuite
3. Bedroom
4. Ensuite
5. Light well to basement
6. Office

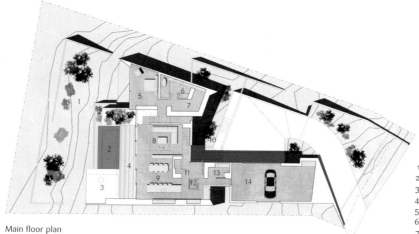

Main floor plan

1. Lower yard
2. Infinity pool
3. Lounge deck
4. Terrace
5. Master bedroom
6. Master ensuite
7. Master closet
8. Living room
9. Kitchen
10. Entrance courtyard
11. Foyer
12. Powder room
13. Laundry
14. Garage

Basement plan

1. Lounge
2. Rec room
3. Entrance courtyard
4. Bedroom
5. Bathroom
6. Storage
7. Ensuite
8. Bedroom

052

Heavily revealed board-formed concrete shows a soft wood grain texture and mimics the natural wood used throughout.

053

Concrete at roof level creates the feeling that the space is solid and sculpted rather than assembled from a series of pieces.

054

The opening created by this massive concrete frame generates a rudimentary connection to the sea and sky. Spaces feel simultaneously open and contained.

This sustainable home celebrates the intersection of earth and sky. One enters below grade and ascends vertically through the ground to arrive in a series of glass pavilions anchored by rammed earth walls and sheltered under kite-like floating roofs. Wood floors, ceilings, and cabinetry provide a sensual layer within the rough walls and surrounding gardens. Ecological responsibility guided the design of this LEED Platinum, net-zero-energy home.

Rammed earth walls use on-site material and provide thermal mass. Lightweight roof planes orient photovoltaics toward the sun, guide rainwater to cisterns, and provide shade through calibrated overhangs. High-efficiency envelope and mechanical systems and graywater recycling further support the ecologically sensitive design.

House of Earth and Sky
7,100 sq ft

Aidlin Darling Design

San Francisco, California, United States

© Matthew Millman

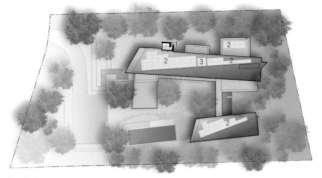

Roof plan

1. Reading tower
2. Photovoltaic panels
3. Solar thermal panels

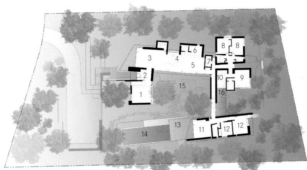

Ground floor plan

1. Game room
2. Upper foyer
3. Living room
4. Kitchen
5. Dining room
6. Office
7. Laundry
8. Kid's bedroom
9. Master bedroom
10. Master bathroom
11. Family room
12. Guest bedroom
13. Deck
14. Swimming pool
15. Terrace
16. Reflecting pond

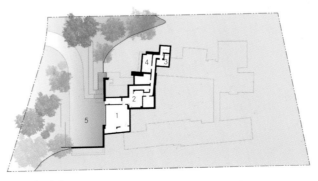

Garage level plan

1. Garage
2. Lower foyer
3. Wine cellar
4. Storage
5. Car court

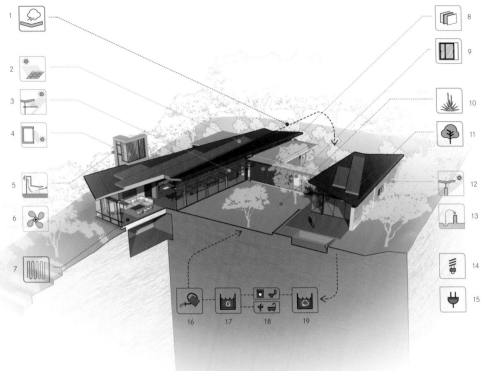

1. Rainwater collection; butterfly roof
2. Photovoltaic and solar thermal panels
3. Horizontal sunshades
4. Vertical sunshades
5. Passive stack ventilation
6. Heat recovery ventilation (HRV) system
7. Radiant heating and cooling
8. High perfomance insulation
9. High perfomance thermally broken windows and doors
10. Drought-tolerant low-irrigation landscape
11. Forest stewardship council (FSC) wood finishes
12. Thermal mass rammed earth walls
13. Site soil used for wall construction
14. 98% of light fixtures are fluorescent or LED
15. All electrical systems; no gas or combustibles
16. Landscape irrigation
17. 500-gallon graywater collection tank
18. Efficiency plumbing fixtures
19. 5,000-gallon rainwater collection tank

Sustainability diagram

The purpose of the sustainability criteria in the construction of this house means a considerable reduction in the environmental footprint, a reduction in costs, and an increase in well-being and comfort.

055

The use of high-quality materials
ensures a home that meets
durability expectations and
maintains its visual appeal.
Maintenance requirements are
another factor that is always
taken into account in sustainable
housing.

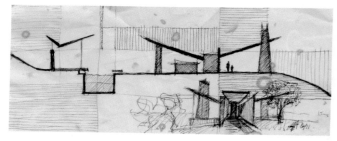

The house has enormous glass enclosures that allow it to be integrated into its natural environment, minimizing the visual impact.

In addition to providing warmth, the use of wood and an earth-tone palette throughout the house ensures a total connection with nature while creating an ideal relaxing atmosphere.

058

The bathtub next to the window overlooking the pond and surrounded by nature makes for an enjoyable bathing experience in this bathroom with a spa soul.

This single-story urban dwelling is designed for a couple and their antique car collection. Through its courtyard scheme, the house gains an inner garden that frames the view of the neighboring preserving trees and, at the same time, provides privacy to the internal spaces.

From outside, the house presents itself as a closed and austere block, whereas from the inner patio, it transforms into transparent, revealing facades.

The dark aesthetic of the exterior materials alludes to the local technique traditionally employed in the treatment of wooden construction, resulting in a simple architecture, fully capable of integrating itself to the surrounding landscape.

Casa de Lata
3,552 sq ft

sauermartins

Canela, Rio Grande do Sul, Brazil

© Federico Cairoli

059

The exterior and interior surfaces combine wood, glass, and metal as a reflection of both industrial and artisanal aspects of the construction process.

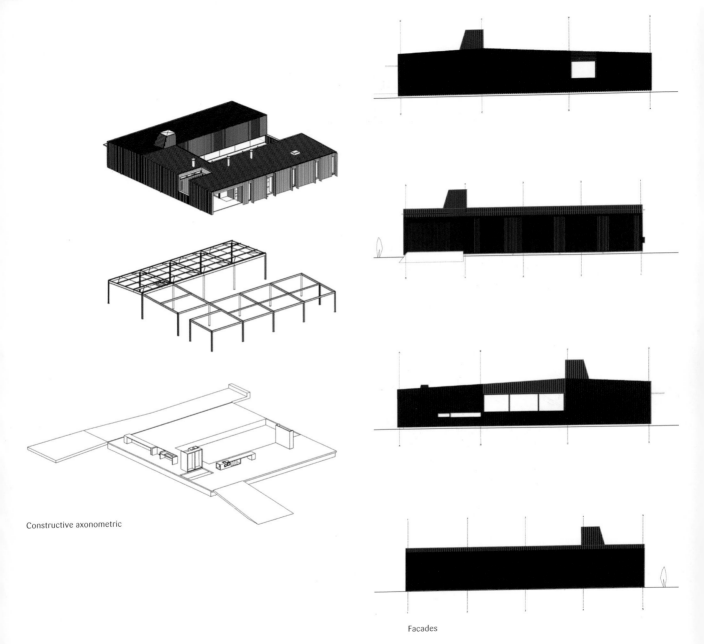

Constructive axonometric

Facades

The square floor plan is divided into
three sectors, resulting in a single-floor
volume. The two sectors are equal in
size and accommodate the garage on
one side and the house on the other.

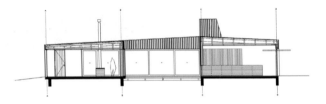

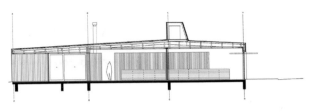

Sections

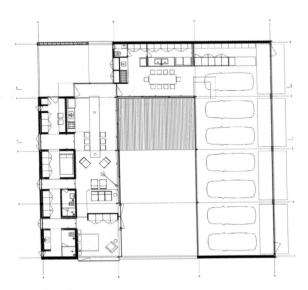

Floor plan

060

The wood of the floor adds warmth and a chromatic contrast to the sober and austere palette of materials of this modern house that celebrates pure and defined lines.

061

Due to its design, its central position as the backbone of the space, and its multiple functions —working area, storage, dining room, woodshed, and fireplace— the concrete island becomes the focal point of the living area.

062

In this bedroom, the views of the garden fill the space with life, as if it were a painting, creating an interesting chromatic contrast with the white that dominates in the room.

Pacific Heights Modern
6,800 sq ft

**Diego Pacheco
Design Practice**

San Francisco, Caliornia,
United States

© Nicolas Gutierrez

The original residence was designed in 1952 by John Bolles,
a prominent San Francisco architect. The structure is a
fine example of Bay Area modernism, with exposed wood
beam ceilings and a mural in the dining area that features a
spectacular cityscape painted by artist Jose Moya del Pino.
In the renovation design, the original spirit of the house was
preserved and the mural was restored, and the historic house
was reorganized around a new central open staircase beneath
an operable skylight. The backyard was transformed into a roof
garden atop an addition that includes a gym, a wine cellar, and
a great room for entertainment. Landscape elements include
mature olive trees, succulents in the private garden, and
colorful maples along the street.

063

In landscape design, trees and
plants should adapt to local climate
and site particulars for successful
plantings.

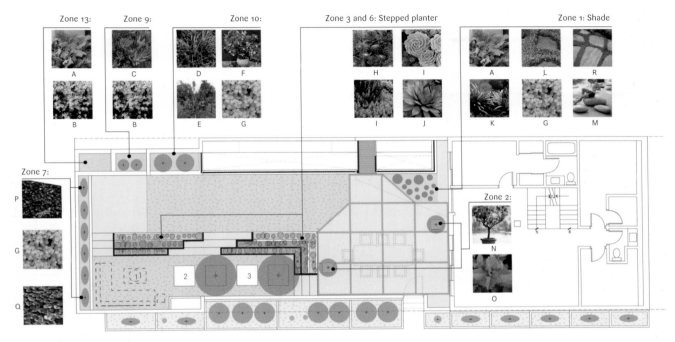

Zone 13:

A

B

Zone 9:

C

B

Zone 10:

D

F

E

G

Zone 3 and 6: Stepped planter

H

I

I

J

Zone 1: Shade

A

L

R

K

G

M

Zone 7:

P

G

Q

Zone 2:

N

O

Planting design. Private garden

1. Firepit
2. Herb garden
3. Water feature

A. Giant chain fern
B. Avalanche
   Evergreen Clematis
C. Icee Blue
D. Apple tree
E. Mondo grass
F. Eureka lemon tree

G. Golden Baby tears
H. Hens and chicks
   succulents
I. Low succulents
J. Medium succulents
K. Dwarf Mondo Grass
L. Blue star creeper

M. Seating
N. Meyer lemon tree
O. Mint
P. Espalier limes
Q. Wild ginger
R. Baby tears

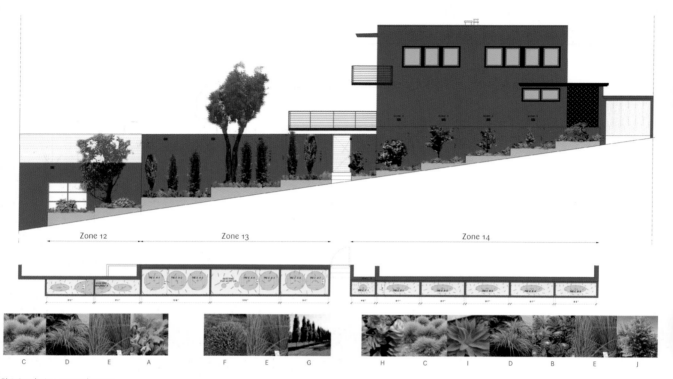

Zone 12   Zone 13   Zone 14

C   D   E   A   F   E   G   H   C   I   D   B   E   J

Planting design, street elevation

A. Giant chain fern
B. Hens and chicks succulents
C. Blue fescue grass
D. Golden Variegated Sweet Flag
E. Juncus Elk Blue
F. Provence lavender
G. Columnar hornbeam trees
H. Variegated String
   of Buttons
I. Agave attenuata
J. Japanese maple

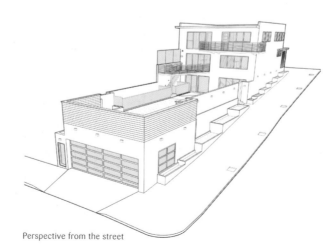

Perspective from the street

The colorful trees planted along the street provide a verdant fence for the house, and at the same time, offers a friendlier sidewalk border for pedestrians.

Upper level floor plan

Main level floor plan

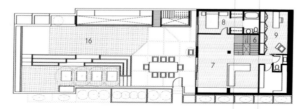

Garden level floor plan

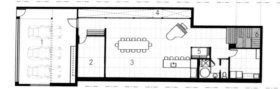

Garage level floor plan

1. Garage
2. Home gym
3. Great room
4. Light well
5. Wine cellar
6. Central stair
7. Playroom
8. Guest suite
9. Office
10. Living room
11. Dining room
12. Kitchen
13. Master suite
14. Office
15. Bedroom
16. Garden

064

Staircases have a strong presence in architecture. Their prominence can be used to create a design statement and a focal point around which spaces are organized.

The custom steel and walnut staircase features an operable louvered screen system. The staircase is topped by a skylight, creating a luminous hub for an active family.

065

An all-white design scheme provides the kitchen with a fresh, modern look. At the same time, white reflects light, making spaces look larger and brighter.

066

Open-tread staircases look lightweight and unobtrusive. When placed under a skylight, they are a good option to allow in maximum natural light.

The garage, far from being considered a residual space, has been built with the same architectural language as the whole house.

This project, in the suburbs of Tel Aviv, houses a young family with three children. Its L-shaped design speaks in a layered language. The owner's basic premise was that she did not want anything to be white, as this reminded her of the clinic where she used to work.

In the beginning of the design process, the architects stripped the house completely and then started to cover it again, taking inspiration from fine fabrics and ornaments. Trees, perforated screens, and curtains were used to create the different layers. This created a beautiful world inside. The light meets the interior, creating a play of projections and reflections. Each surface—the natural wood floors, the ceiling, the walls, the raw concrete—participates in this game in a different but essential way.

Layers
4,844 sq ft

Havkin Architects

Ramat Hasharon, Israel

© Shai Epstein

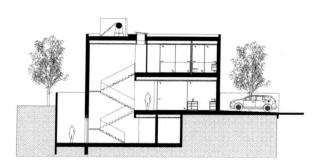

Section BB

First floor plan

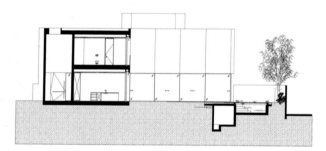

Section 11

Ground floor plan

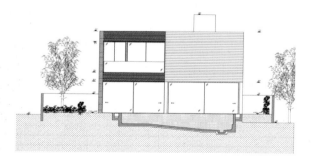

West elevation

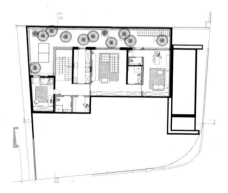

Basement floor plan

067

The Venetian blinds on the windows provide privacy without sacrificing clarity, allowing natural light to enter as needed.

The solidity and roughness of the concrete on the walls contrasts with the lightness of the furniture design, where fine metal sheets serve as shelves and tabletops in the dining room.

The floors of this house are also set in layers. Sometimes it is not clear which floor is ground floor—on one corner of the plot the designated ground floor touches the land. On the opposite corner, it is the basement that does so.

068

The contrast of fuchsia over the muted neutral tones that predominate in the house creates a happy, vital, and energizing atmosphere that speaks of glamour and sophistication.

069

Elegance defines this bathroom clad in black marble. Black and white contrast and complement each other. The combination of both is associated with good taste and quality.

070

At night the house turns into a glowing lantern that marks where the family lives. It influences the atmosphere in the garden and, on a larger scale, impacts the quality of the urban space.

The upper floor is like a weighty box that rests on a glass cube. It encloses the children's domain and the parents' suite. It provides a fitting world of intimacy, security, and privacy.

Carla Ridge
4,000 sq ft

Paul Brant Williger

Beverly Hills, California,
United States

© Mark Angeles

Located in the hills of the Trousdale Estates of Beverly Hills,
this house was originally built in 1959. Before undertaking this
more recent renovation, the entry had been converted into a
bedroom addition, forcing visitors to enter through the carport
into a very tight courtyard. The removal of this bedroom, and
the installation of a large, pivoting front door, restores the
original entrance with heightened drama and grandeur. An
added office off the entry is defined by an angled wall, which
creates a smaller entry space and opens the perspective into
the living room.

This project intends to update the Beverly Hills residence for
the twenty-first century, while maintaining the structure's mid-
century modern spirit.

071

White is the protagonist; it is
present throughout the exterior
and inside on the walls and
furniture. The gray stone, identical
through the entire house,
encourages spatial continuity while
creating a subtle contrast. This
creates a balanced, simple, and
extremely delicate whole.

072

The existing swimming pool, which took up the entirety of the exterior deck, was cut in half. This reduction not only opens up the exterior areas to increase usable space, but also serves as a division that separates the pool from the covered, furnished terrace.

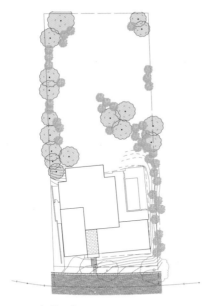

Site plan

Ground floor plan

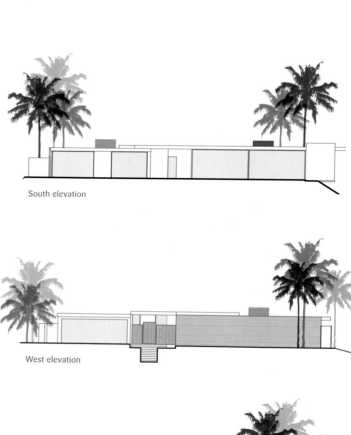

South elevation

West elevation

East elevation

The house is 4,000 square feet, consisting of two bedrooms and a staff room. At the outset of the project, the entire house was stripped down to the wood stud framing for a complete remodel; every surface and finish is new, inside and out.

The kitchen, previously closed off from
the house, now opens up to the living
room, dining room, and sweeping views
of Los Angeles.

073

Surrounded by beautiful views of the mountains, a breakfast room has been designed next to the kitchen. This space, where you can enjoy a quiet morning breakfast, is welcoming and more intimate than the dining room.

074

If space allows, it is a good option to have a complete bathing area: a shower for the busy days and a bathtub reserved for relaxing moments.

The G'Day House is a commission for an expatriate Australian family whose desire was to build a home that would encourage a relaxed attitude to everyday life and help them reconnect with their previous warm-climate lifestyle. The result is an open house, fully connected to the outside world without giving up privacy.

Columnless sliding doors in the southeast corner of the house double the size of the living area when open; the boundaries between inside and outside disappear, making indoor and outdoor spaces an equal priority. Materials, shape, and spatial relationships are designed to evoke the feeling of a beach house: simple, casual, and flexible.

G'Day House
4,400 sq ft

**McLeod Bovell
Modern Houses**

West Vancouver,
British Columbia, Canada

© Ema Peter

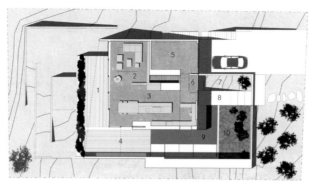

Main floor plan

1. Terrace
2. Living room
3. Kitchen
4. Outdoor cooking
5. Garage
6. Powder room
7. Light well
8. Entry bridge
9. Pond
10. Courtyard/garden

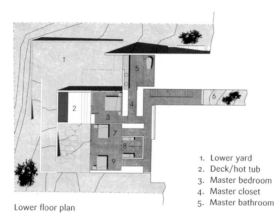

Lower floor plan

1. Lower yard
2. Deck/hot tub
3. Master bedroom
4. Master closet
5. Master bathroom
6. Light well
7. Bedroom
8. Ensuite
9. Bedroom

Basement plan

1. Covered terrace
2. Craft room
3. Rec room
4. Laundry room
5. Bathroom
6. Bar area
7. Bedroom

The cascading walkway leads guests straight to the door, inside to the kitchen, and out to the deck to take in the views.

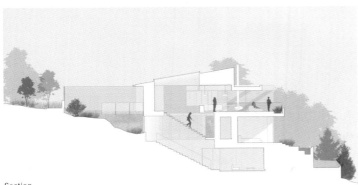

Section

075

A reflecting pond at the outer edge of the house connects this space with an open terrace to the south and an enclosed garden to the north while creating privacy from the street.

076

The dining table and wood-burning fireplace can both be rotated to support a variety of arrangements depending on weather and number of guests.

077

A kitchen island has been designed to allow storage and a bar to have breakfast, a snack, or an informal meal without giving up the impressive views that dominate the living areas of the house.

078

The chromatic palette of materials serves as a connecting thread between all the spaces in the house. The black basalt tile cladding is used in the staircase, the bathroom, and on the wall of the living room, creating an interesting contrast with the clarity of the white and wood that dominate the space.

This new single family home is minimal in form and material, a contemporary counterpoint to the historic fabric of its Cambridge neighborhood that builds on a language of material simplicity and precise assemblage. The building's form shields outdoor living spaces from the public realm of the street and organizes rooms around specific views and direct access to an immersive, lush landscape, managing privacy for its occupants. An intervening micro-courtyard, planted with a single tree, introduces nature and light deep into the living space of the attenuated plan. Daylight washes through interior spaces that are arranged around a figural stair connecting the first floor's open living space to the second floor's bedrooms and studies.

Courtyard House
3,500 sq ft

Anmahian Winton Architects

Cambridge, Massachusetts, United States

© Florian Holzherr and Jane Messinger

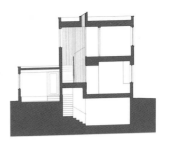

Section S–N through stair

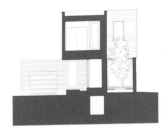

Section S–N through courtyard

Elevations

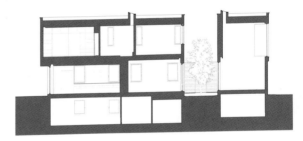

Section W–E through courtyard

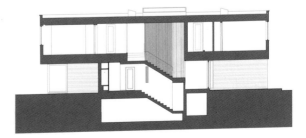

Section E–W through stair

First floor plan

Ground floor plan

The design supports the family's attitude toward environmental stewardship, integrating many sustainable systems and innovative assemblies. Its FSC-certified rainscreen is made of Ipe, a low maintenance/long-life-cycle wood, and is fastened with concealed clips, providing a drainage plane and venting pathways for the building skin. Staggered wall studs afford exceptional depth for open cell insulation, thermal break, and wiring raceway. Ultra-high-efficiency boilers and make-up air exchangers minimize operating costs.

079

The interior patio floods the ground floor with light, making an intimate connection with the interior spaces that are revealed from various angles.

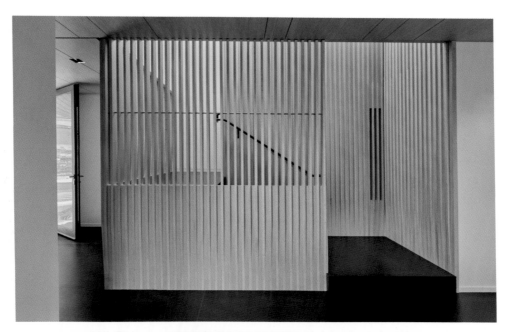

080

In the kitchen it is important to create welcoming and functional lighting that reaches every corner. That's why the lighting of the ceiling has been combined with occasional light from the lamps suspended above the island.

Driven by the client's desire for a characterful home unfamiliar to the sweeping streets of one of Melbourne's most desirable suburbs, the two firms, Tecture and Studio Tate, came together to conceive a family home of both function and flair. Defining Melbourne's bayside aesthetic as largely traditional, the architects imagined an external form that is bold and textured, brought to life with a breadth of timber, brick, and glass. The interior intelligently echoes the exterior, finding inspiration in simple but effective forms that balance pragmatism with personality, and ensure connection, inside and out. This house successfully delivers on its mission to reimagine the possibilities of suburban living, marrying the needs of its family of occupants with architectural significance.

Brighton Residence II
4,897 sq ft

Interior design: Studio Tate
Architecture: Tecture

Melbourne, Victoria, Australia

© Derek Swalwell

First floor plan

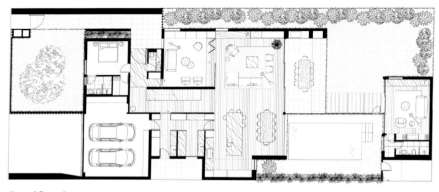

Ground floor plan

This family home houses three
bedrooms, a private guest suite, dual
living zones, a family rumpus room, a
study, an outdoor dining space, a pool,
and a pool house.

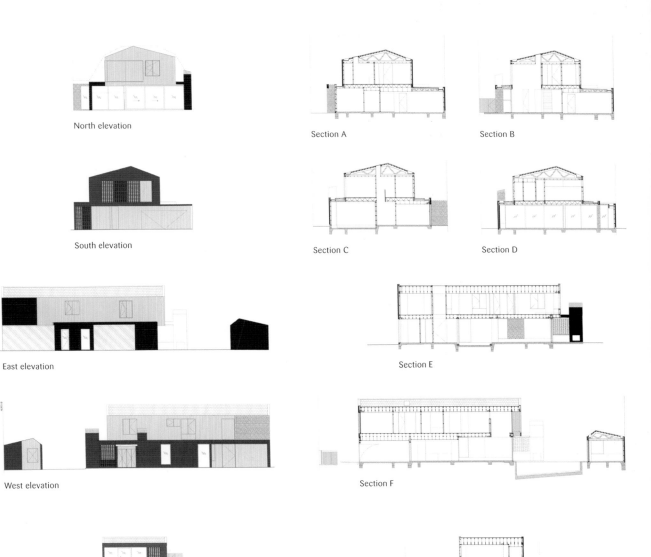

North elevation

South elevation

East elevation

West elevation

Pool house south elevation

Section A

Section B

Section C

Section D

Section E

Section F

Section G

081

The exterior brickwork is mirrored in the living room hearth while additional architectural finishes such as textured wall tiles and graphic terrazzo enhance the sense of harmony.

082

With two adjacent living zones on the ground floor, a sunken lounge in the secondary space encourages intimacy, distinguishing its function from the primary open plan space. Steel-framed fluted glass doors separate the two spaces; a contemporary interpretation of traditional glazed internal passages, and a nod to the recurring themes of pattern and texture.

Brighton Residence II 251

083

Skylights and an immense double-height space above the dining area enhance a connection to the elements, further blurring the line between the interior and exterior, and allowing the residents to bask in the luxury of space.

A high-functioning home for a high-functioning family—comprehensive back-of-house services allow the family to thrive and include laundry, scullery, additional study nook, and children's entry "drop zone."

084

The staircase that leads to the upper floor rests at the entrance of the house on a granite block. The design favors the passage of light as well as the feeling of spatial continuity.

The bathrooms, too, are geometric wonders—a repetitive grid is an alluring backdrop to one's personal needs, be it in the master en suite or shared family bathroom.

Russian Hill

4,816 sq ft

EAG Studio

San Francisco, California,
United States

© Daniel Lunghi and
Prepress Media

From the elegant foyer crowned by a stunning glass chandelier, a wrapped floating oak stairway leads to the top floor of this reverse floor plan featuring expansive northeast views of downtown San Francisco, the Bay Bridge, and Coit Tower. Two peaked skylights and numerous windows on all four levels provide an abundance of natural light throughout the four-bedroom, six-bathroom house. The living wall of the staircase to the panoramic roof deck brings nature to the main floor via a glass wall. A backlit onyx wall highlights the dining room and horizontal straight-grained oak build-ins and wine storage. State-of-the-art security video access, lighting, temperature, and entertainment A/V controls finish this truly smart home.

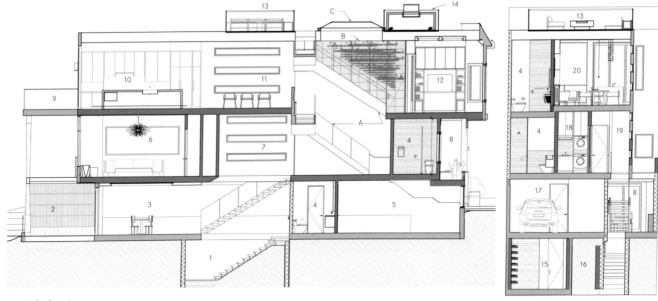

Longitudinal section

1. Staircase to wine
   cellar and gym
2. Courtyard
3. Media room
4. Bathroom
5. Bedroom
6. Master bedroom
7. Hall
8. Foyer
9. Rear deck
10. Kitchen
11. Dining room
12. Library
13. Roof lounge
14. Outdoor kitchen
15. Wine cellar
16. Gym
17. Garage
18. Laundry room
19. Hall
20. Family room
A. Floating staircase with
   glass guardrail
B. Green wall
C. Peaked skylight

Cross section

The layout of the house has been
cleverly adapted to the steep slope
typical of the streets of San Francisco.

085

Living walls create instant visual appeal while bringing nature into the home.

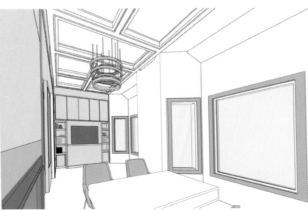

086

The siting and orientation of a building are key factors to take into consideration early on in the design phase, in order to take advantage of natural lighting and views.

087

Openings on more than one wall create rooms where lighting is well-balanced and shadows are minimized.

The owners purchased two lots to develop two spec homes. After going through the design process, they decided to change one of the designs to a custom home for themselves. The only access to the site is from the street, which necessitated the garage to be located at the front of the house. Once accepted as a prominent design element, the garage was used to help define the entry courtyard, and the adjacent home to the east completes the courtyard.

It is a single story house with three bedrooms and two bathrooms and a series of outdoor spaces—entry court, main courtyard, and backyard. The house lays out as a bar running the length of the site, with two wings extending to the east. This provides shading from the western sun in the courtyard during the summer.

Trammel Residence
2,650 sq ft

A.GRUPPO

Dallas, Texas, United States

© Dror Baldinger FAIA
Architectural Photography

The wing closest to the street contains the butler's pantry, kitchen, and living area.

088

The living room has a large, north-facing wall of polycarbonate, which provides diffused lighting throughout the day.

089

The kitchen and living areas are partitioned by a freestanding steel and wood entertainment center. The television is held within this and swivels to face the living room, kitchen, or dining room.

090

The master bedroom wing was conceived of as a box within a box. The central organizing element is a walnut-clad box that contains a small home office, closet, linen storage, WC, and shower. The upper portion of the box is wrapped in polycarbonate to filter natural light from a series of skylights.

091

The flanking wardrobes leading to the vanities on the west wall provide more closet storage.

The floor plan of this single-family house is distributed over four independent volumes that are interconnected by a central patio. A corridor all over the patio's perimeter allows access to the different spaces of the house. The corridor and the patio are separated by a window frame and two walls built with granite stone from the existing structure.

Simplicity was used in the design of the house, which was built using typical materials of Portuguese construction. Inside, the white matte painted plasterboard walls and ceilings exist in harmony with the white lacquered medium-density fiberboard elements, doors, and cabinets.

Casa Galegos
3,552 sq ft

Raulino Silva Arquitecto

Galegos de Santa Maria,
Barcelos, Portugal

© João Morgado

Floor plan

1. Entry
2. Living room
3. Kitchen
4. Bathroom
5. Bedroom
6. Closet
7. Patio
8. Laundry
9. Playroom
10. Office
11. Technical area
12. Garage

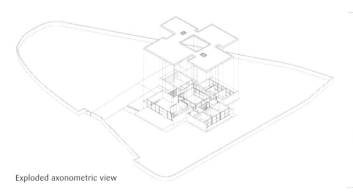

Exploded axonometric view

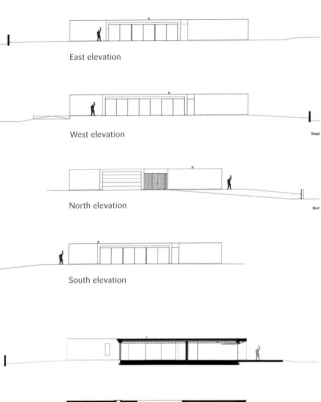

East elevation

West elevation

North elevation

South elevation

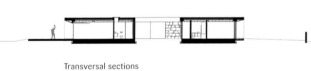

Transversal sections

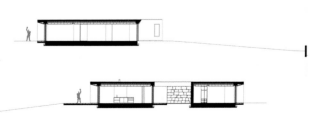

Longitudinal sections

The main entrance, on the north facade, is situated between the garage and the living room and kitchen. The garage, with a technical area and the service WC, faces north. The living room volume extends to the outside through a wood deck flooring, facing west.

092

The entryway to the house, laid with dark gray concrete, was created on the north side of the property, leaving the best solar exposure for the garden.

093

The openings to the outside are lined with porches, extending the interior spaces to the garden and protecting the windows and the exterior shading elements from wind, rain, and solar rays.

094

The white interiors focus on lines
and spaces, and also play with
the light and projected shadows,
enhanced by the use of this color.

The south-facing wing houses the
master bedroom and two children's
rooms, as well as two bathrooms and a
dressing room.

Skyhaus

4,520 sq ft

Aidlin Darling Design

San Francisco, California,
United States

© Matthew Millman

Channeling the spirit of this mid-century modern home's
original designer, the late Joseph Esherick, daylight was a
primary objective for this contemporary transformation.
Central to the new design is a multistoried interior garden
atrium intended to capture outdoor space within the home.
This vast, sky-lit space serves as a spatial hub, pulling daylight
deep into the home's interior. It features a transverse bridge
and a sculpted wood wall that filters and carves light as it
moves through the space.

The dialogue between earth and sky is reinforced through the
home's material palette of concrete, wood, glass, steel, and
diffused light.

095

Choosing a glass barrier without rails for the terrace is a wise choice, as it does not break the aesthetics or affect the design and structure of the building. It provides safety and luminosity, integrating itself as part of the surroundings while allowing the views to be enjoyed without obstacles.

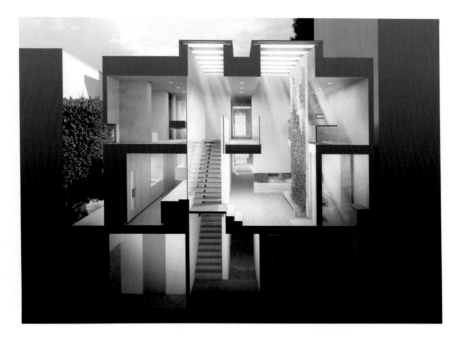

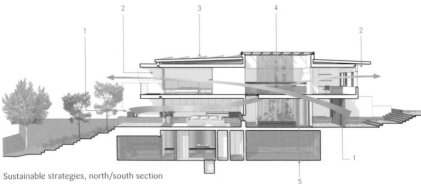

Sustainable strategies, north/south section

1. Ventilation strategies: Large sliding doors open the house along the axis and allow for passive ventilation and cooling on all floors.
2. Daylight control: Operable hurricane shutter system and shades control passive heat gain. Deep overhangs reduce solar heat gain through windows.
3. Renewable energy: Solar photovoltaic rooftop array.
4. Daylight harvesting: Sky-lot atrium provides filtered and refracted daylight to interior, reducing need for artificial lighting and improving interior visual quality.
5. Radiant heating: Energy-efficient hydronic radiant heating in-floor slabs provide heating at occupant level.

096

The home's once dark interior is completely transformed using restrained materials that are intended to reflect, refract, and sculpt light as it is captured.

097

The black-and-white theme runs throughout the house, bringing uniformity to the decoration. The palette of neutral tones is complemented by the ever-present wood to provide a note of warmth and elegance.

098

A home office has been cleverly placed behind the wooden wall. Light is filtered to avoid uncomfortable reflections while also providing much-needed privacy when working.

Elegance combines with modern flavor to create a home full of personality. To bring the scale of the large house down, BeKoM Design created inviting and intimate rooms flooded with natural light while exploring the limitless possibilities of artificial lighting. The design team focused on LED strips to frame the different spaces. This lighting solution provided the spaces with a sophisticated touch and, from a technical point of view, allowed the ceilings to be expressed as clean, continuous surfaces. A palette of warm, light colors combines with a variety of wood finishes and concrete elements to bring warmth and comfort while keeping the decor sleek and simple.

Menlo Park Residence
7,031 sq ft

BeKoM Design

Menlo Park, California,
United States

© Rich Anderson LucidPic

North elevation

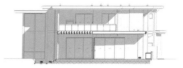

East elevation

South elevation

West elevation

Second floor plan

1. Entry
2. Office/suite
3. Powder room
4. Mudroom
5. Elevator
6. 3-car garage
7. Bedroom suite
8. Media room
9. Pantry
10. Living room
11. Wine room

12. Dining room
13. Great room
14. Outdoor covered patio
15. Outdoor dining area
16. Outdoor kitchen
17. Deck
18. Spa
19. Pool
20. Lawn
21. Natural boulder area
22. Hallway/gallery

23. Laundry room
24. Bedroom suite
25. Bedroom suite
26. Family room
27. Elevator
28. Balcony
29. Bedroom suite
30. Master bedroom
31. Walk-in closet
32. Master bath
33. Master bath balcony

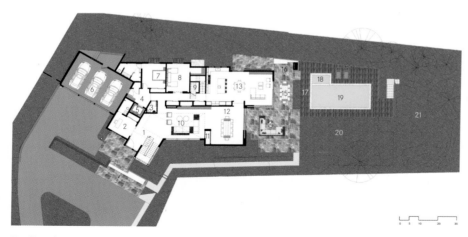

First floor plan

The house occupies the site in an environmentally friendly way, minimizing visual impact while taking advantage of the views and optimizing outdoor living.

Terraces are sheltered beneath roofs, taking advantage of the views. The generous use of glass softens the indoor-outdoor boundaries and allows abundant natural light into the house.

099

Inherently modern, floor-to-ceiling windows are essential construction elements that offer limitless design possibilities. They expand the limits of the house to the outdoors and bring in light and views.

100

Artificial lighting, like natural lighting, can transform the atmosphere of a room. They both have an effect on spatial perception and mood.

Artificial lighting complements natural light through various creative design solutions that add visual interest.

101

The selection of the adequate type and amount of lighting should adapt to different situations and activities while contributing to the creation of inviting environments.

102

Modern white spaces glow in
the light, lending a sense of
expansiveness and airiness.

The House in Mishref is home to two brothers and their families, who have varying lifestyles and needs for privacy and open spaces. An introverted composition of two separate living units grouped around an internal courtyard, the house is an interpretation of the traditional courtyard house.

Presenting a clean and serene facade to the street, the structure manifests as a white monolithic volume poised elegantly on top of a stone cladded podium. The rhythmic arrangement of louvered windows across the facade softens the volume by lending it a sense of lightness. The calming sound of water from the courtyard fountain and the diffused light filtered through the louvered windows make this house an oasis of tranquility in this busy Kuwaiti suburb.

House in Mishref
15,069 sq ft

Studio Toggle
Mishref, Kuwait
© João Morgado

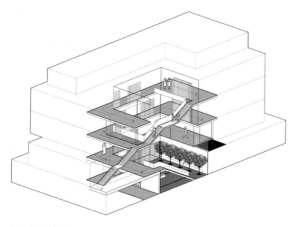

Circulation loop

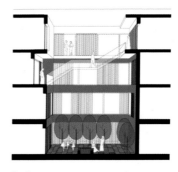

Section

Courtyard void

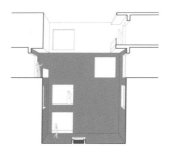

Social and climatic significance
of courtyard and fountain

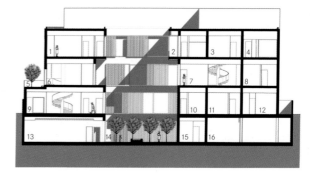

Building section

1. Living and dining rooms (house 2)
2. Bedroom 1 (house 2)
3. Bedroom 2 (house 2)
4. Master bedroom (house 2)
5. Balcony (house 1)
6. Family living room (house 1)
7. Family living room (house 2)
8. Bedroom 3 (house 2)

9. Living and dining rooms (house 1)
10. Bedroom 1 (house 1)
11. Bedroom 2 (house 1)
12. Master bedroom (house 1)
13. Diwaniya
14. Courtyard
15. Driver's room
16. Parking

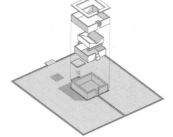

Fountain exploded axonometric view

103

The courtyard and the open-air space results in an inward-looking typology that can benefit from maximum diffused daylight without compromising on privacy.

Second floor plan

1. Living and dining rooms
2. Guest bathroom
3. Open kitchenette
4. Kitchen
5. Laundry
6. Clothes drying room
7. Maid's room
8. Storage
9. Master bedroom
10. Balcony
11. Bedroom 1
12. Bedroom 2
13. Lobby
14. Stair
15. Elevator

Roof floor plan

1. Exterior deck
2. Pool
3. HVAC
4. Pool technical area
5. Water tanks
6. Lobby
7. Elevator

Ground floor plan

1. Parking access ramp
2. Entrance
3. Living and dining room
4. Guest bathroom
5. Open kitchenette
6. Kitchen
7. Laundry
8. Clothes drying room
9. Maid's room
10. Master bedroom
11. Bedroom 3
12. Bedroom 4
13. Bedroom 5
14. Open to sky patio
15. Stair
16. Elevator
17. Courtyard below

First floor plan

1. Family living room
2. Open kitchenette
3. Storage
4. Office
5. Living room
6. Open kitchenette
7. Bedroom 6
8. Bedroom 7
9. Bedroom 8
10. Stair

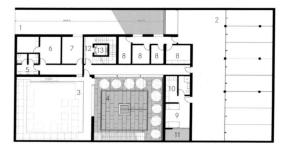

Basement plan

1. Parking access ramp
2. Parking
3. Diwaniya
4. Courtyard
5. Guest bathroom
6. Pantry and silver room
7. Prayer room
8. Storage
9. Driver's room
10. Pantry
11. Patio
12. Lobby
13. Elevator

104

In addition to its aesthetic value as the center of attention in the room, the spiral staircase allows the two floors to be connected by a much smaller space than a traditional staircase would occupy.

105

In this large living area, the chaise longue makes use of the space by adapting to the length of the wall and also offers an extra area for sitting or lying down.

The interior of the house features a
simple palette of ethereal white and
natural woods. The straight and minimal
lines of the rooms are offset by the
sleek curves of spiral staircases.

106

The furniture has been carefully chosen to contrast with the serene atmosphere without breaking with the modern and minimalist style that characterizes the house's design.

107

A large suspended stair is key to an architectural promenade that sweeps through all the floors, offering vantage points and ease of access.

On the roof, an external area of decking and a pool shaded by metal louvers provides dramatic views out over the city.

Facing into the courtyard, areas of glazing have been shielded with black louvers to create gradations in privacy and light levels for the interiors.

Dogtrot

3,500 sq ft

CLB Architects

Jackson, Wyoming, United States

© Matthew Millman,
    Audrey Hall

This residence combines simplicity with interest. The design references its rural surroundings and is based on the concept of a dogtrot barn, two separate but connected forms housing the residence and the garage. The roof of the main structure is asymmetrically gabled. Although the house is one gabled form, protected outdoor spaces are carved out of the main structure and extended on either end, where perforated siding adds texture and provides covered porches with privacy and shelter.

Drama is a constant factor—in the sense of space created by the width and span of the connector roof; in the entry, with its oversized pivoting door flanked by glass; in the way the interiors open up to the views; and in bold and whimsical interior details—creating the perfect venue for a dynamic couple's retirement years.

The house sits on a quiet 18-acre
meadow lot boasting 360-degree views
of ranchlands, foothills, and Glory Peak
just outside Jackson, Wyoming.

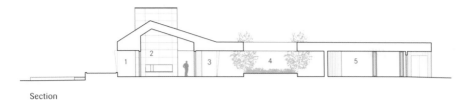

Section

1. Covered terrace
2. Living space
3. Covered terrace
4. Covered entry
5. Garage

Main floor plan

1. West terrace	10. Guest bedroom
2. Master bedroom	11. Office/bunk
3. Master bathroom	12. East terrace
4. Covered terrace	13. Reflecting pool
5. Great room	14. Living terrace
6. Entry	15. Garage
7. Mud/gear/laundry	16. Planter
8. Gallery	17. Bocce court
9. Map room	18. Potting shed

108

The long rectangular residence (160' x 37') is connected to a separate garage structure by a three-foot thick roof. There, a large central cutout lightens the mass, creates a focal point, and causes a dynamic play of light upon the corresponding scaled planter below it.

109

Throughout, materiality is minimal. The exterior is clad in oxidized steel, the interiors expressed in steel, glass, and concrete. The only wood used is larch—warm, light, and rustic in character—and in places it wraps up the walls to the ceiling and continues outside.

110

The main objective was to
make this modern space warm,
welcoming, and livable. Artifacts
and whimsical objects, such as
taxidermy specimens from the
owners' collection, imbue the
space with personality.

111

In the powder room, an energizing abstract design, derived from brain scans, on an orange background injects interest and vitality into the small space.

Originally built in 1925, this two-story residence stands on an oak-studded property facing a meadow. Andrew Mann Architecture and Niche Interiors joined forces to create an airy, light-filled, and spatially rich home that connects with its natural surroundings. The contemporary update employs simplified traditional forms that highlight the home's original character. The remodel improves the circulation patterns through the house, connecting the spaces to one another. It also develops strong linear axes favoring visual connection between interior spaces and minimizing indoor-outdoor boundaries through large-paned windows and French doors opening directly to wooden decks.

Meadow Estate
6,400 sq ft

Architects: Andrew Mann Architecture

Interior design: Niche Interiors

San Francisco Peninsula, California, United States

© Paul Dyer

White-painted wood trellises overhead
shade the seating and dining areas while
filtering and modulating the sunlight
that streams into the house.

The overall design creates a vocabulary
of elements with careful detailing, clean
lines, and a color palette of whites,
grays, and blues.

112

Hallways, vestibules, and mudrooms all offer endless design possibilities for designers and homeowners to explore, from creative storage solutions to surfaces for art display.

Skylights direct sunlight to accentuate important interior nodes and draw in the eye, while illumination from these openings brightens otherwise dark areas.

113

Kitchens have evolved from being a tucked-away room in a corner to a crucial gathering space within the home. In this home, the fluidity of the kitchen and dining and living areas become essential gathering spots and in essence the heart of the house.

114

The design of contemporary homes
generally promotes fluid circulation
patterns between different rooms.
Good connections between rooms
bring sightlines into focus, making
the home feel open and airy.

Thompson House
5,000 sq ft

splyce design

West Vancouver,
British Columbia, Canada

© Sama Jim Canzian

Located on a steep site in West Vancouver, the Thompson House was designed to capture views of the port in one direction and mountains in the other, while controlling sightlines to and from the neighbors on either side.

Like the wings of a bird stretched out to protect its young, the two side walls and roof on the south elevation extend far past the exterior walls, providing privacy and large covered decks. The cedar-clad wing walls block any visual distraction of the adjacent properties and focus the view from the interior toward the ocean. The roof structure is undulating and pinwheel-like, resulting in a different slope on each of the four exterior elevations and, consequently, varied ceiling heights on the upper-floor interior: low in the bedrooms, high in the circulation zone.

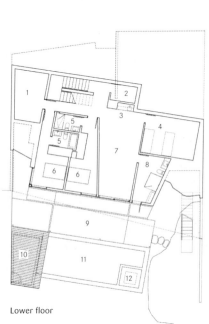

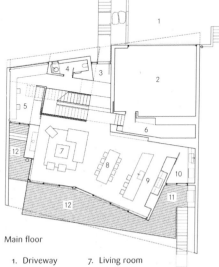

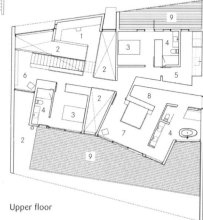

Lower floor

1. Mechanical
2. Wine cellar
3. Bar
4. Media room
5. Bathroom
6. Bedroom
7. Rec room

8. Bathroom/
   changing room
9. Patio
10. Deck
11. Pool
12. Hot tub

Main floor

1. Driveway
2. Garage
3. Entry
4. Powder room
5. Office
6. Mudroom

7. Living room
8. Dining room
9. Kitchen
10. Wok kitchen
11. BBQ deck
12. Deck

Upper floor

1. Study
2. Open to below
3. Bedroom
4. Bathroom
5. Laundry

6. Library
7. Master
   bedroom
8. Dressing room
9. Deck

Upon entry into the home, space rises up and momentarily draws attention away from the straight-shot ocean view ahead and upward toward the wall-to-wall skylight and exposed heavy timber rafters—a stark contrast to the rest of the light-colored materials in the palette.

115

The covered deck spaces are extensions of the interior and invite various uses throughout the year.

116

While the house is porous, open,
and social, it is also nuanced, with
layers and nooks that provide
areas of retreat and solitude. A
private office tucked behind the
staircase can suddenly change
character and be part of the
adjacent living space by way of an
unexpected sliding wall panel.

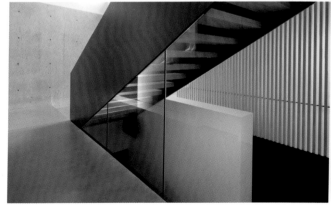

117

In this house, the opening of floor plans as well as the visual connection between the different floors offer opportunities for interaction between family members.

118

The wooden closets that define
this luminous kitchen compensate
for the starkness of the white and
gray, contributing the warmth and
serenity of a noble material and
creating a balanced and simple
pattern that is repeated throughout
the house.

Two bridges offer opportunities for spontaneous interaction and play, as family members cross and engage with those below.

119

The beds have been orientated
so the spectacular views can be
enjoyed in full. Unlike the living
areas, where the floor is made of
polished concrete, the bedrooms
have wooden floors to make
these spaces warmer and more
welcoming.

The primary design goal for this home was to capture the lavish lake and mountain views afforded by the site, while taking into consideration possible future development with potential to impede the view. The design solution places living spaces on the top floor, ensuring the view, and incorporates an elevator shaft allowing for aging in place. The three levels are shifted rather than stacked neatly on top of one another. This strategy reduces the apparent scale of the home, provides a dramatic covered entry experience, and creates a roof terrace off the living/dining spaces. The home's strong street presence and bold modernity responds to a neighborhood context rich with excellent examples of mid-century modern architecture.

View Ridge
3,000 sq ft

Heliotrope Architects

Seattle, Washington, United States

© Haris Kenjar

120

Significant existing trees and shrubs were leveraged in the design, creating a rich entry experience and a strong connection to nature from both the entry and the upper floor.

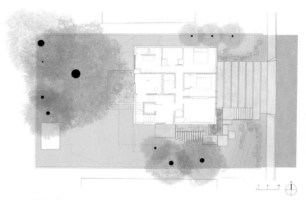

Site plan

Garage and support spaces are placed
below grade, with the second floor
entry flush with the above grade portion
of the site.

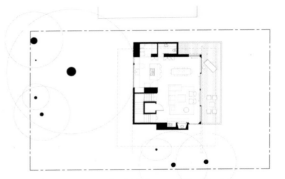

Third level plan

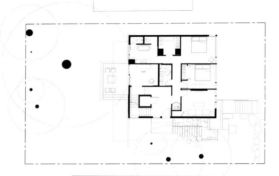

Second level plan

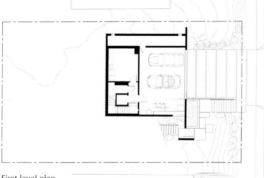

First level plan

Section

The glass wall creates the sensation of enjoying the relaxing experience of bathing in the midst of nature.

121

The kitchen island, in addition to being used as a cooking area, also functions as an informal dining space away from the more formal dining room.

122

The sofas in the living room have been positioned so that you can enjoy the views outside. A small space overlooking the staircase has been used to house a secluded office area.

Sonoma Retreat

2,900 sq ft

Architects: Andrew Mann Architecture

Interior Design: Angus McCaffrey Interior Design

Sonoma County, California, United States

© David Wakely

This weekend getaway for busy professionals looking to unwind and connect with nature creates a relaxing environment. While iconic and modern in form, the home—originally built in 1974—was in need of an interior refresh. A thoughtfully planned kitchen, new bathrooms and stairs, as well as new lighting and casework throughout create a new "heart of the home." The renovation also enhances the outdoor experience through the creation of a new vegetable garden and pavilion. The pavilion's shed roof evokes the rural architecture of Northern California, while the symmetrical curves of the garden beds, which respond to the existing topography, blend into the landscape to create a lush architectural framework.

Everything from materials to lighting
choices were selected to create a
modern yet relaxed ambience.

123

Contemporary home design promotes fluid circulation patterns and the creation of sightlines that connect spaces and enrich the spatial experience.

124

Architectural design is generally enhanced by the thought-out use of natural lighting and sightlines that frame views.

The renovation also focused on the creation of an outdoor experience. For the new garden pavilion, the hardscape and layout of the fences and surrounding planter beds were designed to create a peaceful and harmonious garden experience.

The overall result is a sensational wine country getaway that allows the family to feel, at all times, the deep connection to the stunning natural surroundings.

125

House designs extend past the doorstep to the outdoors. This garden and its pavilion reinforce the aesthetic concept of the overall design.

126

An outdoor dining pavilion can be perfect for entertaining during the good-weather months. Cozy furniture and an efficient cooking area provides the comforts of an indoor cooking experience, while guests can enjoy the open air.

Butterfly Residence
2,900 sq ft

Feldman Architecture

Carmel, California,
United States

© Joe Fletcher Photography
   and Jason Liske

This house is a retreat befitting the natural beauty of a hilly site covered with native grasses and studded with oak, redwood, and pine trees. The clients were meticulous in the selection of the site, searching for two years for a spectacular piece of land that was flat enough to accommodate living on one level. Sitting lightly on the land, the house is divided into three pavilions that are topped by expressive butterfly roofs. The distinctive roof shapes are a take on the client's vision of butterflies alighting on the meadow site. The pavilions are modest in size, yet each expands into an outdoor room opening up to dramatic views of the canyon below and the hills above. The house uses little energy as a result of extensive day lighting and passive thermal strategies.

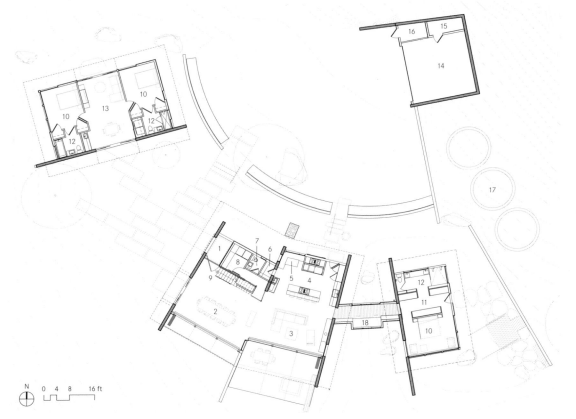

Floor plan

1.	Entry	10.	Bedroom
2.	Dining room	11.	Dressing room
3.	Living room	12.	Bathroom
4.	Kitchen	13.	Family room
5.	Nook	14.	Garage
6.	Pantry	15.	Wine cellar
7.	Powder room	16.	Garbage
8.	Laundry room	17.	Water tanks
9.	Stairs to media loft	18.	Office

Each pavilion has a separate function: the central pavilion houses the main living, dining, and cooking spaces, while the other two pavilions provide for sleeping, bathing, and relaxing.

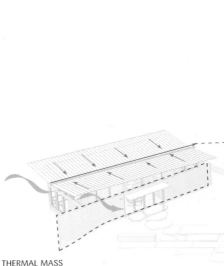

SOLAR ELECTRICITY
HARVESTING
The south-facing garage
roof harvests solar energy
on a 7kw solar array.

WATER HARVESTING
Butterfly roofs carefully channel rainwater in two
directions, spilling over in a dramatic waterfall
onto splash pads below. The water is then piped
up to three concrete water tanks. 30,000 gallons
of collected rainwater help irrigate the restored
meadow of native grasses and wildflowers.

THERMAL MASS
Board-formed concrete walls and
concrete floors serve as heat sink to keep
temperatures well-regulated. Radiant floor
heating in concrete floors keep the building
warm in the winter with less energy. Walls
help absorb excess solar heat to keep
interiors cool.

PASSIVE SOLAR (WINTER)
A south-facing window wall allows light
and heat to penetrate on winter days.

PASSIVE COOLING (SUMMER)
Deep awnings and roof overhangs
block out the hotter, steeper summer
solar energy. Strategically placed
windows provide cross ventilation in
all pavilions. Thermal mass in concrete
walls also helps absorb excess
daytime heat in the summer.

Sustainability diagram

Water is celebrated throughout the
design. Each roof funnels water to a
rain chain fountain and into landscape
collection pools, which then gather in
cisterns where the water is stored and
used to irrigate the landscape.

The design of the house integrates
indoor and outdoor spaces with a
modern, simple aesthetic and provides
separate spaces for the growing family.

127

Garden benches, firepits, and
stylish patio furniture perfectly
shape outdoor space to make
the most of the outdoor living
experience.

128

Clerestory windows add to the
architectural appeal of a building,
especially when combined with
spans of walls to create interesting
combinations of planes—some
transparent, others opaque.

The use of concrete and large expanses of glass openings acts as a heat sink, absorbing heat from the sunlight all day and releasing that heat at night.

129

Clerestories on the sunny side of a
building should be protected from
sunlight in the summer by deep roof
overhangs, to avoid overheating.

Double Bay

7,211 sq ft

SAOTA

Sydney, New South Wales,
Australia

© Adam Letch

Set on a north-facing cove in Sydney's vast natural port, the building appears as a collection of planes; a play on space, privacy, and threshold. Graphite gray sail screens are rigged just off the house, providing privacy from the road. Timber cladding, plastered mass walls, a wood-clad soffit, and the exaggerated sill of a bay window punched through the sail screens are layered into further planes. This play creates depth in an otherwise linear facade and provides privacy while optimizing light and views of the park.

A playful character, the calculated blurring of boundaries, and the fresh, layered composition bring into balance the domestic needs of a young family and the wow factor that this phenomenal site deserves.

130

A timber roof canopy connects the street side to the garden and the beach. It permeates the interior, presenting itself at odd moments, and it protects and defines the collection of internal and external spaces composed beneath.

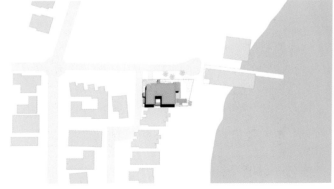

Site plan

131

The house has a U-shaped plan. The entrance is a link between two wings, separated by an internal garden, which, like an internal port, allows views through the spaces to the bay beyond.

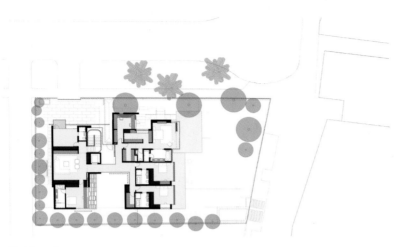

First floor plan

Ground floor plan

132

The bayside wing of the house is
one open-plan space. Stairs, rather
than walls, delineate the raised
kitchen and family dining room
from more formal areas.

133

The stairwell is fully glazed but wrapped protectively in a cloak of timber louvers. This gently curved outline contrasts with the surrounding crystalline box and mediates between the formal entrance and the bedrooms above.

Materials were carefully chosen to site the house. The use of wood, white walls, and travertine floors reflect the seaside setting.

134

Echoing the entrance and the staircase, a slatted wooden panel separates part of the kitchen from the outside, providing privacy without losing light and ventilation.

Designed to fit the site's landscape and blend with the local architectural vernacular, three structures—main house, guest house, and barn—on a 75-acre lot in Columbia County, New York, resolve contradictions to provide a home for a young family of four.

In the main house, two sections—one a wood-sided rectangle and the other a shingled pitched roof structure—intersect to create an interesting contrast of textures. The barn and the guest house are two separate wooden spaces. Both are visible in the distance from the main house terrace, activating the meadows between them, yet each structure claims ownership of a separate outdoor area of the property—the house and barn own the meadows, the guest house the woods leading to the river.

House in the Hudson Valley

Main house 6,000 sq ft
Guest house 900 sq ft
Barn 2,000 sq ft

Rangr Studio

Columbia County,
New York, United States

© Michael Biondo

The wood-sided section contains a large garage, guest bedrooms, and a playroom and can be closed off from the shingled structure, which contains the family bedrooms and main living spaces.

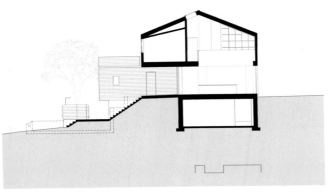

Section

First floor plan

Ground floor plan

The main house includes two garages,
seven bedrooms, and four living areas
yet feels like an intimate home.
The compound uses geothermal energy
for heating and cooling, with efficient
heat pumps that greatly reduce the
need for fossil fuel energy.

135

A covered outdoor terrace
overlooks a long pool and provides
a panoramic view unobstructed by
columns. Stone steps lead down
to the pool and continue into it,
reminiscent of ancient stepwells
found in India.

136

Due to their spectacular design, the dining room lamps become the indisputable protagonists of this space, filling it with personality and style while serving to clearly delimit the dining area.

137

A balcony connecting the
bedrooms overlooks a double-
height living and dining area, giving
the owners a view of the whole
house, which greatly contributes to
the feeling of intimacy.

The contrast of textures enriches the
decoration without giving up chromatic
uniformity.

A separate guest house for long-term visitors is limited to 900 square feet by local zoning ordinances, but contains two bedrooms, a living/dining/kitchen area, and a large wrapping screen porch nestled in the trees with a view. It is within earshot of the river that borders the property.

Guest house floor plan

A barn is located in another meadow on the property. It creates space for activities in inclement weather and holds a large PV solar array.

This residence is located on a secluded site on the banks of the Snake River. Drawing inspiration from the adjacent braided and ever-changing river channels, the precise layout of this house creates a unique relationship to the site from each room, as well as dynamic views and spatial experiences.

The sequence of interior spaces gradually unfolds to reveal near and distant features of this natural environment. Large window walls in primary spaces connect interior and exterior seamlessly while private areas provide framed access to views. The gray and wood-texture exterior rain screen creates continuity with the surrounding cottonwood forest. The house lends itself in color and form to the nearby fabric of river islands.

River Channel Residence

15,000 sq ft

Dynia Architects

Jackson Hole, Wyoming, United States

© Dynia Architects

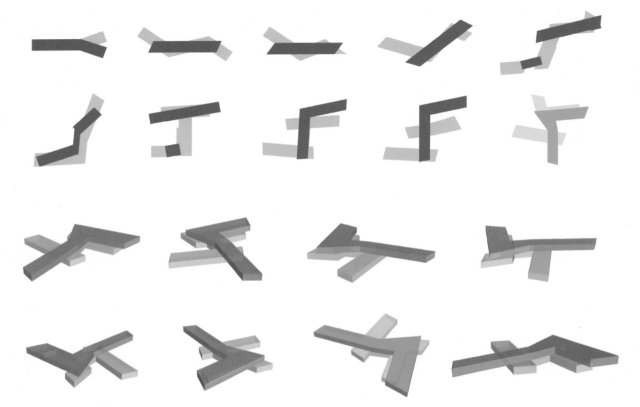

Diagrammatic progression

The rigorous design process started with stacked linear elements that began to shear and shift in response to an evolving, complex program in the context of a site with multiple focuses: contemplative pond, rushing river, majestic mountain range, and intimate cottonwood forest.

138

The primary wing cantilevers boldly toward the river to provide the most inclusive views for the master bedroom while creating covered outdoor dining below.

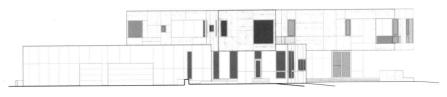

South elevation

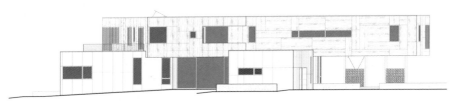

West elevation

North elevation

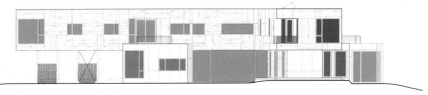

East elevation

The overall form is composed of three major rectilinear volumes that intersect and shift according to the family's desire to have expansive views of the river.

Second level plan

Basement plan

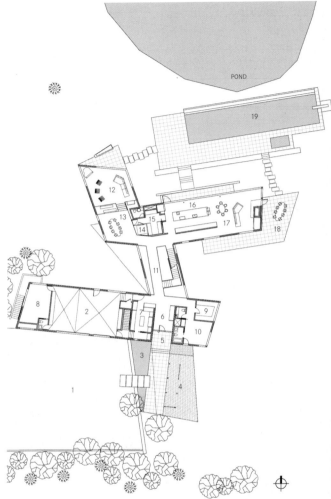

POND

First floor plan

1. Parking court	10. Yoga	19. Pool	28. Mechanical
2. Garage	11. Stair atrium	20. Game room	29. Storage
3. Water feature	12. Living room	21. Deck	30. Office
4. Sculpture garden	13. Dining room	22. Bunker room	31. Laundry
5. Entry patio	14. Elevator	23. Sitting	32. Wine
6. Entry	15. Pantry	24. Wardrobe	33. Rec room
7. Mudroom	16. Kitchen	25. Bath	
8. Exercise	17. Family	26. Bedroom	
9. Study	18. Outdoor dining	27. Theater	

139

A secondary bedroom wing, supported on thin columns, extends into the landscape and creates cover for the main entry while framing a view of the riverscape beyond.

The simplicity of the surfaces on the inside, with a clear predominance of white, in contrast to the color and texture of the natural environment, makes them the perfect backdrop for displaying and giving prominence to works of art.

140

Fluidity of space is encouraged.
The arrangement of the furniture,
as well as the lighting, defines the
different environments without the
need to separate them and lose
the visual connection.

141

A three-story atrium brings light into the core of the house, connects a below grade level with the floors above, and creates transition from the public to the private zones.

This relaxing oasis for an intercontinental couple and their two young children blurs indoors and outdoors, while referencing elements of their mixed heritage throughout the design. Located in a neighborhood of similarly scaled homes, near Silicon Valley's intellectual and financial hub, the house features an H-shaped plan that maximizes its 10,893-square-feet lot size. The material palette features a variety of environmentally sustainable wood species: the facade for the two-story main section is western red cedar, while the flanking one-story sections are made from smooth-troweled integral color stucco. This massing opens up in the rear of the house through fully retractable floor-to-ceiling glass doors to an Ipe deck courtyard and surrounding garden.

Butterfly House
4,898 sq ft

William Duff Architects

California, United States

© Matthew Millman

Rear elevation

Front elevation

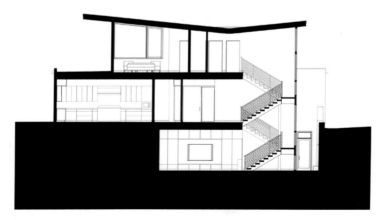

Section

142

The sides of the courtyard are clad in accordion glass doors and courtyard decking is installed at nearly the same level as the adjacent interior floors, so that one can flow freely from inside to out.

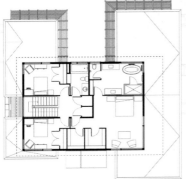

Second floor plan

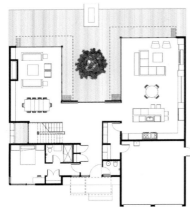

First floor plan

Basement plan

Site plan

1. House
2. Deck
3. Firepit
4. Arbor

There is ample space for entertaining, including formal and informal living spaces, an expansive courtyard for an indoor/outdoor connection, a chef's kitchen and wine cellar, and a media room.

Internal spaces feature a similarly layered palette of fumed-oak wood floors, stained vertical-grain Douglas-fir paneling, stained Tay Koto veneer cabinets, and a stained white oakwood stair.

143

The open staircase expands the home's visual space while giving the illusion of structural lightness, providing greater luminosity and offering a play of light and shadow to the area. The interconnected glass wall provides spatial continuity and visual connection between the spaces.

144

In keeping with the sustainable
material palette found throughout
the house, the living room and
bedrooms utilize natural fabrics and
fibers such as linen, wool, cotton,
or rattan. Collectively, these fabrics
are proven to be healthier choices
for both the environment and those
who use them.

River's Reach
10,000 sq ft

Architecture: [STRANG]

Interior Design: DKOR Interiors

Fort Lauderdale, Florida,
United States

© Claudio Manzoni

River's Reach represents an evolution of tropical modern
design, fusing fundamental concepts of the Sarasota School of
Architecture, updated for today's lifestyle. The South Florida
home is notable for its advancement of the movement's
timeless concepts, which were pioneered by several of Florida's
renowned mid-century architects, including Paul Rudolph,
Alfred Browning Parker, and Rufus Nims. As such, the home
features concrete slabs elevated above the ground in search of
breezes, views, and safety. In addition to impressive spans and
cantilevers, the home also offers a striking appearance due to a
collection of vertical "fins" that provide both sun-shading and
privacy elements. Located on Fort Lauderdale's New River, a
special emphasis was placed on enabling an outdoor lifestyle.

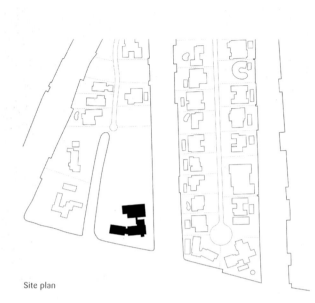

Site plan

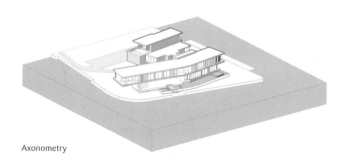

Axonometry

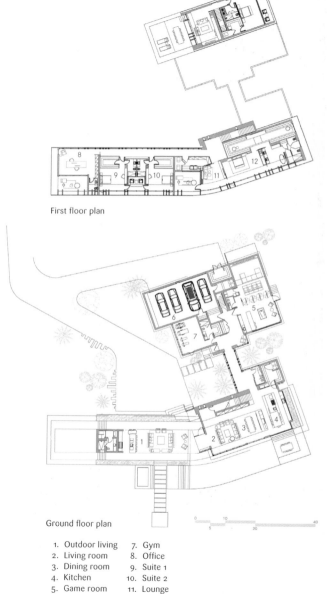

First floor plan

Ground floor plan

1. Outdoor living
2. Living room
3. Dining room
4. Kitchen
5. Game room
6. Garage
7. Gym
8. Office
9. Suite 1
10. Suite 2
11. Lounge
12. Master suite

145

The climatic conditions must determine the architecture, the form, the distribution, the type of construction, and in many cases the materials used to provide comfortable and cozy spaces.

Axonometric view

146

Thanks to the skylight (above), natural light reaches the depths of the staircase, which at night is illuminated by cleverly placed LED lighting under the railing, which guides the way.

147

In this semi-open bedroom, the slatted wooden paneling frames the bed like a headboard, creating a more welcoming and beguiling visual focus. In the same way, a similar panel system in the bathroom achieves privacy for the bathtub area without breaking the flow of the space.

This resort-inspired home in Bali's iconic surf destination, Uluwatu, puts a contemporary spin on local materiality and vernacular architecture to create a luxurious modern holiday home deeply attuned to its beautiful surroundings.

The house sits on a large east–west oriented site facing the ocean on the eastern side. The scale of the site allows for the design to accommodate a resort-inspired layout, with separate suites and living spaces in a fragmented arrangement that weaves together indoor and outdoor spaces. A series of courtyards, gardens, and other planted terraces are deftly woven into the architecture, combining structured and naturalistic planting and creating a sense that landscape and architecture are meaningfully integrated.

Uluwatu
20,053 sq ft

SAOTA

Bali, Indonesia

© Adam Letch

148

A large palm-lined entry courtyard creates a dramatic sense of arrival with a grand staircase floating over a cascading water feature. Monolithic stone-clad walls add a singular design statement to the experience of entering the house.

Site plan

Throughout the plan, large spaces such as the entrance, pool terrace, and western courtyard are balanced with intimately proportioned living spaces.

A lounge, dining room, and covered terrace form the core of the cellular arrangement of buildings and pavilions, which radiate outward, organically interspersed with planted courtyards and terraces. A large courtyard to the west provides an enclosed counterpoint to the vast views to the east.

First floor plan

Ground floor plan

1. Dining room
2. Lounge
3. Covered terrace
4. Cocktail bar
5. Dining pavilion
6. Bedroom suite
7. Study
8. Cinema room
9. Kitchen
10. Cigar lounge
11. Laundry
12. IT/Server
13. Storage
14. Staff quarters
15. Garage
16. Guard house
17. Services
18. Pool plant

A range of covered outdoor spaces and courtyards, pavilions, and terraces offer a variety of outdoor experiences with varying degrees of cover.

149

The porous nature of the design encourages naturally cooling cross ventilation to flow in from the ocean. When the heat becomes oppressive, it's possible to retreat into the fully enclosed, air-conditioned lounge and dining areas.

150

The eye-catching slope of the roof is a climatically appropriate response to the east–west orientation of the house, inviting in the morning light and opening up ocean views to the east, while providing shelter from the harsh afternoon light from the west.

Vertical screens, joinery, and decorative
metalwork, such as the faceted bronzed
aluminium behind the bar and in the
cigar lounge, enrich the raw materiality
with thoughtful details.

Honed and unfilled travertine floors provide a luxurious finish underfoot while the continuity of the finishes imparts a sense of calmness and cohesion. High-quality imported European furnishings and finishes introduce a sense of understated luxury with a contemporary take on pared-back mid-century design.

DIRECTORY

57STUDIO
Santiago, Chile
57studio.com

A.GRUPPO
Dallas, Texas, United States
agruppo.com

Aidlin Darling Design
San Francisco, California, United States
aidlindarlingdesign.com

Andrew Mann Architecture
San Francisco, California, United States
andrewmannarchitecture.com

Angus McCaffrey Interior Design Inc.
Sausalito, California, United States
angusmaccaffrey.com

Anmahian Winton Architects
Cambridge, Massachusetts, United States
aw-arch.com

BAM! Arquitectura
San Isidro, Buenos Aires, Argentina
bamarquitectura.com

BeKoM Design
Cupertino, California, United States
bekomdesign.com

Brewster McLeod
Aspen, Colorado, United States
brewstermcleod.com

CLB Architects
Jackson, Wyoming, United States
clbarchitects.com

Diego Pacheco
San Francisco, California, United States
diegopacheco.com

DKOR Interiors
Miami, Florida, United States
dkorinteriors.com

Dynia
Jackson, Wyoming, United States
Denver, Colorado, United States
dynia.com

EAG Studio
San Francisco, California, United States
eagstudio.com

Feldman Architecture
San Francisco, California, United States
feldmanarchitecture.com

Guy and Ian Ayers/Moody Studio
Los Altos Hills, California, United States
dguyayers.com

Ground Studio
Monterey, California, United States
groundstudio.com

Havkin Architects
Ramat HaSharon, Israel
havkinh.com

Heliotrope Architects
Seattle, Washington, United States
heliotropearchitects.com

Jeanne Moeschler Interior Design
Menlo Park, California, United States
jeannemoeschler.com

JFAK
Los Angeles, California, United States
www.jfak.net

McLeod Bovell Modern Houses
Vancouver, British Columbia, Canada
mcleodbovell.com

Niche Interiors
San Francisco, California, United States
nicheinteriors.com

Paul Brant Williger
Beverly Hills, California, United States
willigerarchitect.com.

Pete Moffat Construction
Palo Alto, California, United States
petemoffat.com

Rangr Studio
New York, New York, United States
Berkeley, California, United States
rangr.com

Raulino Silva Arquitecto
Vila do Conde, Portugal
raulinosilva.blogspot.com

Renato D'Ettorre Architects
Darlinghurst, New South Wales, Australia
dettorrearchitects.com.au

SAOTA
Cape Town, South Africa
saota.comt

sauermartins
Porto Alegre, Brazil
sauermartins.com

splyce design
Vancouver, British Columbia, Canada
splyce.ca

[STRANG]
Miami, Florida, United States
Sarasota, Florida United States
Fort Lauderdale,Florida, United States
strang.design

Studio Tate
Richmond, Victoria, Australia
studiotate.com.au

Studio Toggle
Salmiya, Kuwait
Porto, Portugal
studiotoggle.com

Swatt I Miers Architects
Emeryville, California, United States
swattmiers.com

Tecture
Collingwood, Victoria, Australia
tecture.com.au

The Ranch Mine
Phoenix, Arizona, United States
theranchmine.com

William Duff Architects
San Francisco, California, United States
wdarch.com